ALGEBRA 1
Workbook

350+ Practice Problems
and Review Prep

Table of Contents

Order of Operations

When solving equations with multiple operations, special rules apply. These rules are known as the **Order of Operations**. The order is as follows: Parentheses, Exponents, Multiplication and Division from left to right, and Addition and Subtraction from left to right. A popular mnemonic device to help remember the order is Please Excuse My Dear Aunt Sally (PEMDAS).

Evaluate the following problems using the order of operations:

1 $4 + (3 \times 2)^2 \div 4$

_____

2 $2 \times (6 + 3) \div (2 + 1)^2$

_____

3 $2^2 \times (3 - 1) \div 2 + 3$

_____

4 $(12 + 3) \times (8 - 2) - 5^2$

_____

5 $(19 - 8) \times (13 - 3) + 2^2$

_____

6 $(2 + 4)^2 + (9 + 12 \div 4)$

_____

7 $3 \times (13 \times 3 + 8^2) - 12$

_____

8 $[(4 + 3)^2 + 1] + 2^3 - 5$

_____

9 $[6^2 + (20 \div 5 + 4^2)] \div 7$

_____

10 $(15 \div 5)^2 - [(12 + 2) + 3^2]$

_____

Translating Algebraic Expressions

An algebraic expression is a statement about an unknown quantity expressed in mathematical symbols. The statement "five times a number added to forty" can be expressed as $5x + 40$. When expressing a verbal or written statement mathematically, it is vital to understand words or phrases that can be represented with symbols. The following are examples:

Symbol	Phase
+	Added to; increased by; sum of; more than
-	Decreased by; difference between; less than; take away
X	Multiplied by; 3(4,5...) times as large; product of
÷	Divided by; quotient of; half (third, etc.) of
=	Is; the same as; results in; as much as; equal to
x,t,n, etc.	A number; unknown quantity; value of; variable

Translate the following verbal statements into mathematical expressions:

1 5 less than 9 times k

_____

2 12 is added to the product of b and 4

_____

3 a squared plus the product of 7 and d

_____

4 Subtract 9 from 3 times p and divide the result by 2

_____

5 2 times the sum of 8 and r

_____

6 Three-fifths z times the difference of y and 1

_____

7 The difference of x times 4 and 14 times y squared

_____

8 2 less than the sum of one-fifth of g and two-thirds of m

_____

9 One-half of g is added to the quotient of 10 and a

_____

10 15 more than the product of d and 2 less than v

_____

2

Evaluating Algebraic Expressions

Given an algebraic expression, you may be asked to evaluate for given values of variable(s). In doing so, you will arrive at a numerical value as an answer.

For example: Evaluate $a - 2b + ab$ for $a = 3$ and $b = -1$

To evaluate an expression, the given values should be substituted for the variables and simplified using the order of operations. In this case: $(3) - 2(-1) + (3)(-1)$. Parentheses are used when substituting.

Evaluate the following algebraic expressions for the given values.

1 What is the value of
$x^2 - 2xy + 2y^2$ when $x = 2$, $y = 3$?

_____

2 What is the value of
$8n + 5n^3 + 16n^2$ when $n = 4$?

_____

3 What is the value of
$(15 - 8t^2) - (5g^3 - 9 + 6g^2) + (3 + 7t)$
when $t = -2$, $g = 7$?

_____

4 What is the value of
$(2a^2 + 6a^4 - 4a)(3b^3 + 8b^2 + b)$
when $a = 3$, $b = -6$?

_____

5 What is the value of
$9k^2 - 6l^2 + 8k$ when $k = 12$, $l = -8$?

_____

6 What is the value of
$(8b^2 + 3) + (58 - 2b^3) - (6b^3 + 4b)$
when $b = 2$?

_____

7 What is the value of
$(8c^3 - 6c^2 + 4) + (3d^3 + 7c^2)$
when $c = -4$, $d = 3$?

_____

8 What is the value of
$y(9 - 7x^4 + 2x)$ when $x = -3$, $y = 7$?

_____

9 What is the value of
$(8 + 4c^2) - (2d^3 - 3d^2)$ when $c = 15$, $d = 4$?

_____

10 What is the value of
$(2m^2 + 3)(4n^2 - 7n)$ when $m = 1$, $n = -1$?

_____

Solving Equations

When asked to solve a linear equation, it requires determining a numerical value for the unknown variable. Given a linear equation involving addition, subtraction, multiplication, and division, isolation of the variable is done by working backward. Addition and subtraction are inverse operations, as are multiplication and division; therefore, they can be used to cancel each other out.

The first steps to solving linear equations are to distribute if necessary and combine any like terms that are on the same side of the equation. Sides of an equation are separated by an = sign. Next, the equation should be manipulated to get the variable on one side. Whatever is done to one side of an equation must be done to the other side to remain equal. Then, the variable should be isolated by using inverse operations to undo the order of operations backward. Undo addition and subtraction, then undo multiplication and division. For example:

Solve: $4(t - 2) + 2t - 4 = 2(9 - 2t)$

Distribute: $4t - 8 + 2t - 4 = 18 - 4t$

Combine like terms: $6t - 12 = 18 - 4t$

Add 4t to each side to move the variable: $10t - 12 = 18$

Add 12 to each side to isolate the variable: $10t = 30$

Divide each side by 10 to isolate the variable: $t = 3$

The answer can be checked by substituting the value for the variable into the original equation and ensuring both sides calculate to be equal.

Solving Equations Exercises

Solve each equation for the unknown variable.

1 $4x - 3 = 5$

_____

2 $6x + 4 = 16$

_____

3 $\sqrt{1 + x} = 4$

_____

4 $\dfrac{x + 2}{x} = 2$

_____

5 $3x - 4 + 5x = 8 - 10x$

_____

6 $\dfrac{2x}{5} - 1 = 59$

_____

7 $25 = 5(3 + x)$

_____

8 $12 = 2(3x + 4)$

_____

9 $8 = 5(3 + 6x)$

_____

10 $8 + 5x = 3(2 - 9x)$

_____

11 $-6 = 10(4x + 3)$

_____

12 $2 - 6x = 3 + 4(5 - 9x)$

_____

13 $10 - 9x = 3 + 4(6 - 2x)$

_____

14 $4x = 7(2x + 10)$

_____

15 $12 = 2(x^2 - 11) + 2$

_____

16 $3(15 - 2x) = (x - 3)^2$

_____

17 $\sqrt[3]{2x + 11} + 9 = 12$

_____

18 $\dfrac{x^2 + x - 30}{x - 5} = 11$

_____

Adding and Subtracting Polynomials

When adding or subtracting polynomials, each polynomial should be written in parenthesis; the negative sign should be distributed when necessary, and like terms need to be combined. Here's a sample equation:

add $3x^3 + 4x - 3$ to $x^3 - 3x^2 + 2x - 2$. The sum is set as follows:

$$(x^3 - 3x^3 + 2x - 2) + (3x^3 + 4x - 3)$$

In front of each set of parentheses is an implied positive 1, which, when distributed, does not change any of the terms. Therefore, the parentheses should be dropped and like terms should be combined:

$$x^3 - 3x^2 + 2x - 2 + 3x^3 + 4x - 3$$
$$4x^3 - 3x^2 + 6x - 5$$

Simplify each of the following expressions by adding or subtracting the polynomials and collecting like terms.

1. $(x^3 - 3x^2 + 2x - 2) - (3x^3 + 4x - 3) =$

2. $(5x^2 - 3x + 4) - (2x^2 - 7) =$

3. $(7n + 3n^3 + 3) + (8n + 5n^3 + 2n^4) =$

4. $(9 - 7x^4) - (2x^4 + 3) =$

5. $(8 + 4d^2) - (2d^3 - 6 - 3d^2) =$

6. $(2m^2 + 3) - (4m^2 - 7 + m^4) =$

7. $(4 - 8t^2) - (5t^3 - 9 + 6t^2) + (3 + 7t) =$

8. $(2a^2 + 6a^4 - 4a) - (3a^2 + 8a^3 + a) + (7a^3 - 5a^4 - 9a^2) =$

9. $(2k - 5k^4) + (7k + 4k^3) - (9k^3 - 6k^4 + 8k) =$

10. $(8b^5 + 3) + (5b^5 + 8 - 2b^3) - (6b^3 + 4b) =$

11. $(2 - 9c^3 + 5c^4) - (8c^4 - 6c^2 + 4) - (3c^3 + 7c^2) =$

12. $(5a^2 - 7a + 2) - (8a - 9) + (4a^4 + 6a^2 + 3) =$

Multiplying Monomials and Polynomials

When multiplying monomials, the coefficients are multiplied and exponents of the same variable are added. For example:
$$-5x^3y^2z \times 2x^2y^2z^3 = -10x^2y^0z^4$$

When multiplying polynomials, the monomials should be distributed and multiplied, then any like terms should be combined and written in standard form. Here's a sample equation:
$$2x^3(3x^2 + 2x - 4)$$

First, $2x^3$ should be multiplied by each of the three terms in parentheses:
$$2x^3 \times 3x^2 + 2x^3 \times 2x + 2x^3 \times -4$$
$$6x^{3+2} + 4x^{3+1} - 8x^3$$
$$6x^5 + 4x^4 - 8x^3$$

Multiplying binomials will sometimes be taught using the FOIL method (where the products of the first, outside, inside, and last terms are added together). However, it may be easier and more consistent to think of it in terms of distributing. Both terms of the first binomial should be distributed to both terms of the second binomial. For example, the product of binomials $(2x + 3)(x - 4)$ can be calculated by distributing 2x and distributing 3:
$$2x \times x + 2x \times -4 + 3 \times x + 3 \times -4$$
$$2x^2 - 8x + 3x - 12$$

Combining like terms yields:
$$2x^2 - 5x - 12.$$

Multiplying Monomials and Polynomials Exercises

Simplify the following expressions by multiplying.

1. $6(3r - 4) =$

2. $12(3x^2 + x) =$

3. $y^2(y + 15) =$

4. $5x(x + 4) =$

5. $2(7x^2 + 3x - 8) =$

6. $4x^2(-x + 3) =$

7. $6x(7x^2 - 3x + 1) =$

8. $(x^2 + 3x - 1)(5x^3 - 2x^2 + 2x + 3) =$

9. $(x + 2)(x - 3)(x - 3) =$

10. $2x^2(7x^2 - 9x + 2) =$

11. $3x(x^2 + xy + 4y^2) =$

12. $6x^3(3x^2 + 2xy + 5y^2) =$

13. $(4x + 2)^2 =$

14. $(x + 4)^2 =$

15. $(x - 5)(x + 5) =$

16. $(6x - 9)(6x - 9) =$

17. $(8x + 3)^2 =$

18. $(x + 2)(x^2 + 5x - 6) =$

Multiplying Polynomials Using the FOIL Method

FOIL is a technique for generating polynomials through the multiplication of binomials. FOIL is an acronym for First, Outer, Inner, and Last. "First" represents the multiplication of the terms appearing first in the binomials. "Outer" means multiplying the outermost terms. "Inner" means multiplying the terms inside. "Last" means multiplying the last terms of each binomial.

After completing FOIL and solving the operations, like terms are combined. Like terms are those with the same variable and the same exponent. For example, in $4x^2 - x^2 + 15x + 2x^2 - 8$, the $4x^2$, $-x^2$, and $2x^2$ are all like terms because they have the variable (x) and exponent (2). Thus, after combining the like terms, the polynomial has been simplified to $5x^2 + 15x - 8$.

Ultimately, the purpose of the FOIL method is to simplify an equation involving multiple variables and operations.

Use the FOIL method to multiply the following monomials, binomials, and/or polynomials. After doing so, be sure to simplify, where possible, by combining like terms:

1 $(x + 10)(x + 4) =$

2 $(x - 2)(x + 8) =$

3 $(x - 3)(x + 12) =$

4 $(x + 15)(x - 1) =$

5 $(x + 10)(x + 6) =$

6 $(x - 4)(x + 9) =$

7 $(x - 7)(x - 5) =$

8 $(x + 8)(x + 1) =$

9 $(x + 6)(x + 3) =$

10 $(x - 10)(x - 2) =$

Factoring

To factor an expression, a greatest common factor needs to be factored out first. Then, if possible, the remaining expression needs to be factored into the product of binomials. A binomial is an expression with two terms.

Greatest Common Factor

The greatest common factor (GCF) of a monomial (one term) consists of the largest number that divides evenly into all coefficients (number part of a term); and if all terms contain the same variable, the variable with the lowest exponent. The GCF of $3x^4 - 9x^3 + 12x^2$ would be $3x^2$. To write the factored expression, every term needs to be divided by the GCF, then the product of the resulting quotient and the GCF (using parentheses to show multiplication) should be written.
For the previous example, the factored expression would be: $3x^2(x^2 - 3x + 4)$

Factoring Ax² + Bx + C When A = 1

To factor a quadratic expression in standard form when the value of a is equal to 1, the factors that multiply to equal the value of c should be found and then added to equal the value of b (the signs of b and c should be included). The factored form for the expression will be the product of binomials: (x + factor1)(x + factor2). Here's a sample expression: $x^2 - 4x - 5$. The two factors that multiply to equal c(-5) and add together to equal b(-4) are -5 and 1. Therefore, the factored expression would be (x - 5)(x + 1). Note (x + 1)(x - 5) is equivalent.

Factoring a Difference of Squares

A difference of squares is a binomial expression where both terms are perfect squares (perfect square - perfect square). Perfect squares include 1, 4, 9, 16... and x^2, x^4, x^6 ... The factored form of a difference of squares will be:
($\sqrt{\text{term1}}$ + $\sqrt{\text{term2}}$)($\sqrt{\text{term1}}$ - $\sqrt{\text{term2}}$)
For example: $x^2 - 4 = (x + 2)(x - 2)$ and $25x^2 - 81 = (5x + 9)(5x - 9)$

Factoring Ax² + Bx + C when A ≠ 1

To factor a quadratic expression in standard form when the value of a is not equal to 1, the factors that multiply to equal the value of a × c should be found and then added to equal the value of b. Next, the expression splitting the bx term should be rewritten using those factors. Instead of three terms, there will now be four. Then the first two terms should be factored using GCF, and a common binomial should be factored from the last two terms. The factored form will be: (common binomial) (2 terms out of binomials). In the sample expression $2x^2 + 11x + 12$, the value of a × c is (2 × 12) = 24. Two factors that multiply to 24 and added together to yield b(11) are 8 and 3. The bx term (11x) can be rewritten by splitting it into the factors: $2x^2 + 8x + 3x + 12$. A GCF from the first two terms can be factored as: 2x(x + 4) + 3(x + 4). A common binomial from the last two terms can then be factored as: 2(x + 4) + 3(x + 4). The factored form can be written as a product of binomials: (x + 4)(2x + 3).

Factoring Exercises

Factor each of the following quadratics.

1 $(b^2 - 5b) =$

_____

2 $(x^2 - 16) =$

_____

3 $(t^2 + 4t) =$

_____

4 $k^2 - k - 56 =$

_____

5 $t^2 + 11t + 18 =$

_____

6 $(5a^2 + 5a) =$

_____

7 $(t^2 - 3t) =$

_____

8 $a^2 + 7a + 12 =$

_____

9 $3w^2 - 12w - 135 =$

_____

10 $(a^2 - 9) =$

_____

11 $5p^2 + 5p - 150 =$

_____

12 $40c^2 - 36c - 36 =$

_____

13 $(100y^2 - 36) =$

_____

14 $3g^2 + 12g - 36 =$

_____

15 $(25x^2 - 64) =$

_____

16 $16y^2 - 60y + 56 =$

_____

17 $6r^2 + 31r + 40 =$

_____

18 $30v^2 - 105v - 135 =$

_____

19 $6d^2 + 2d - 28 =$

_____

20 $24f^2 + 12f - 36 =$

_____

Finding Zeros of Polynomials

To find the zeros of a polynomial function, it should be written in factored form, then each factor should be set equal to zero and solved. To find the zeros of the function $y = 3x^3 - 3x^2 - 36x$, the polynomial should be factored first. Factoring out a GCF results in: $y = 3x(x^2 - x - 12)$

Then factoring the quadratic function yields: $y = 3x(x - 4)(x + 3)$
Next, each factor should be set equal to zero: $3x = 0$; $x - 4 = 0$; $x + 3 = 0$.
By solving each equation, it is determined that the function has zeros, or x-intercepts, at 0, 4, and -3.

Find the zeros of the following polynomials:

1 $y = (3x - 2)(x - 3)$

2 $y = (3x - 5)(x + 5)$

3 $y = 5x^2 - 39x + 28$

4 $y = x^3 + 4x^2 + 4x$

5 $y = (x^2 + x - 20)$

6 $y = x^3 - 3x^2 - 4x$

7 $y = (20x^2 - x - 12)$

8 $y = (10x^2 - 19x - 15)$

9 $y = (x^3 + 5x^2 - 2x - 24)$

10 $y = (x^3 + 2x^2 - 9x - 18)$

11 $y = (x^2 - 7x + 12)$

12 $y = (25x^2 - 30x + 8)$

13 $y = (12x^2 - 25x + 12)$

14 $y = (x^3 + 12x^2 + 47x + 60)$

15 $y = (25x^2 + 10x - 8)$

Finding Slope from Coordinate Pairs

Use the two coordinate pairs to calculate the slope of a linear equation that would pass through both points. Recall that rate of change for any line calculates the steepness of the line over a given interval. Rate of change is also known as the slope or rise/run. The slope of a linear function is given by the change in y divided by the change in x. So, the formula looks like this:

$$\text{slope} = \frac{y_2 - y_1}{x_2 - x_1}$$

1 **(3, -4) and (5, -2)**

slope:
_____

2 **(4, -3) and (-2, -7)**

slope:
_____

3 **(3, 0) and (5, 4)**

slope:
_____

4 **(-1, -4) and (-2, 2)**

slope:
_____

5 **(2, -5) and (3, 5)**

slope:
_____

6 **(-7, -7) and (7, 7)**

slope:
_____

7 **(3, 1) and (-3, -3)**

slope:
_____

8 **(4, 4) and (1, 5)**

slope:
_____

9 **(-5, 2) and (5, 3)**

slope:
_____

10 **(3, -5) and (5, 5)**

slope:
_____

Finding Linear Equations from Graphs

Given the graph of a line, its equation can be written in two ways. If the y-intercept is easily identified (is an integer), it and another point can be used to determine the slope. When determining $\frac{change\ in\ y}{change\ in\ x}$ from one point to another on the graph, the distance for $\frac{rise}{run}$ is being figured. The equation should be written in slope-intercept form, $y = mx + b$, with m representing the slope and b representing the y-intercept. The equation of a line can also be written by identifying two points on the graph of the line. To do so, the slope is calculated and then the values are substituted for the slope and either of the ordered pairs into the point-slope form of an equation.

Determine the equation of each line graphed on the coordinate plane.

1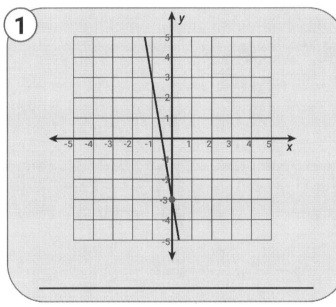

2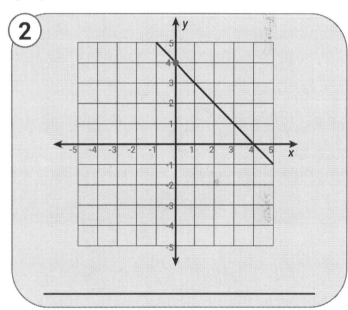

3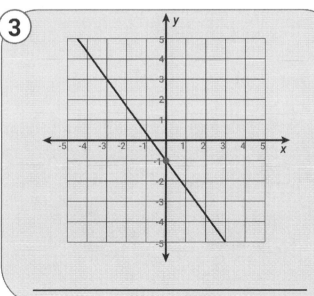

4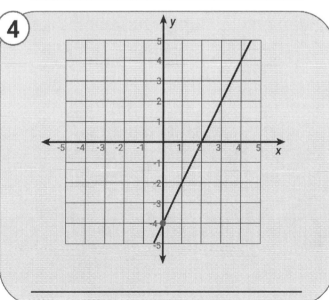

5

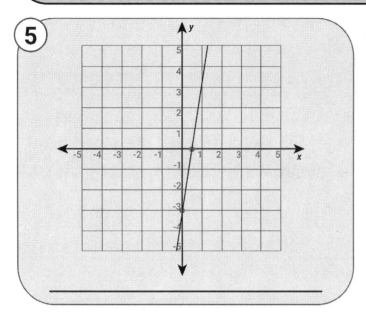

_____

6

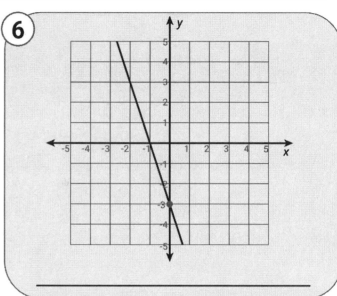

_____

7

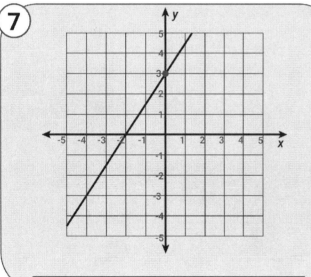

_____

8

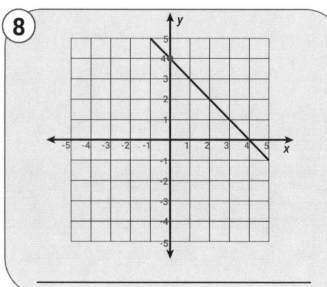

_____

9

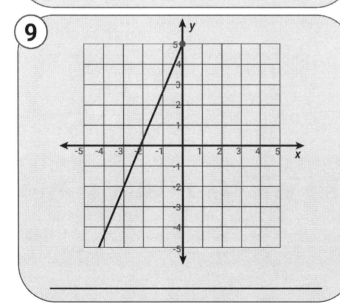

_____

10

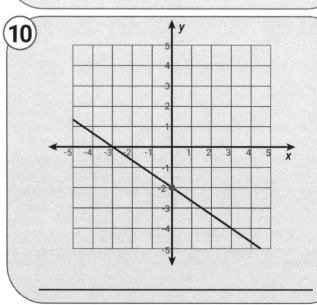

_____

11

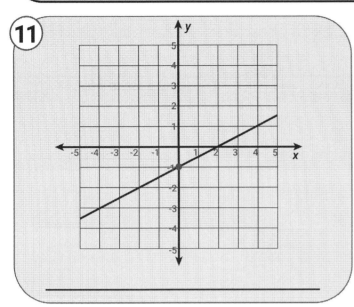

_____

12

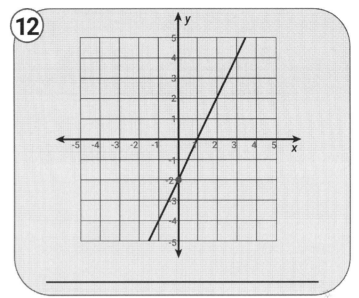

_____

13

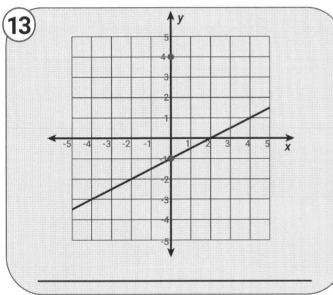

_____

14

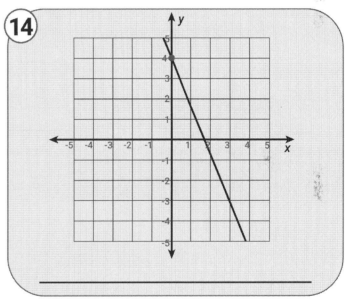

_____

15

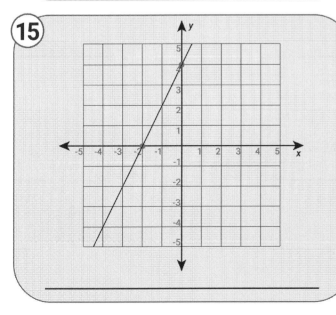

_____

16

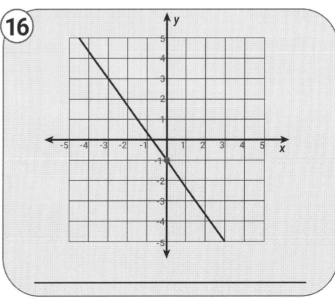

_____

17

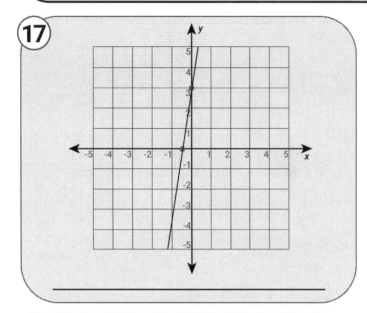

_____

18

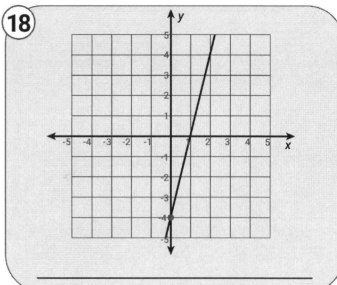

_____

19

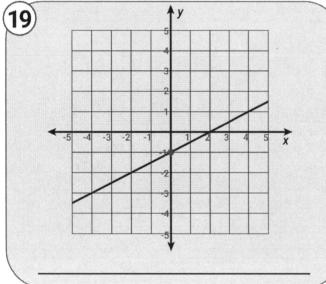

_____

20

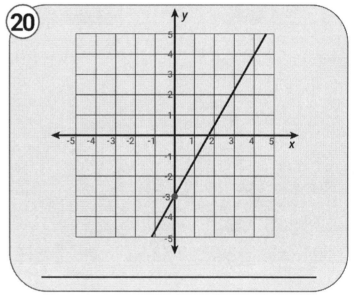

_____

Graphing Linear Equations

When an equation is written in slope-intercept form, $y = mx + b$, m represents the slope of the line and b represents the y-intercept. The y-intercept is the value of y when x=0 and the point at which the graph of the line crosses the y-axis. The slope is the rate of change between the variables, expressed as a fraction. The fraction expresses the change in y compared to the change in x. If, when the run is 1, the rise is an integer, the slope will be written as that integer instead of a fraction with a denominator of 1. For example, if the rise is 5 and the run is 1, the slope can be written as 5.

To graph a line given an equation in slope-intercept form, the y-intercept should plotted first. For example, to graph $y = \frac{2}{3}x + 7$, the y-intercept of 7 would be plotted on the y-axis (vertical axis) at the point (0, 7). Next, the slope would be used to determine a second point for the line. Note that all that is necessary to graph a line is two points on that line. The slope will indicate how to get from one point on the line to another. The slope expresses vertical change (y) compared to horizontal change (x) and therefore is sometimes referred to as $\frac{rise}{run}$.

The numerator indicates the change in the y value (move up for positive integers and move down for negative integers), and the denominator indicates the change in the x value. For the previous example, using the slope of $-\frac{2}{3}$, from the first point at the y-intercept, the second point should be found by counting down 2 and to the right 3. This point would be located at (3, 5).

When an equation is written in standard form, $Ax + By = C$, it is easy to identify the x- and y-intercepts for the graph of the line. Just as the y-intercept is the point at which the line intercepts the y-axis, the x-intercept is the point at which the line intercepts the x-axis. At the y-intercept, x=0; and at the x-intercept, y=0. Given an equation in standard form, x=0 should be used to find the y-intercept. Likewise, y=0 should be used to find the x-intercept. For example, to graph 3x + 2y = 6, 0 for y results in 3x + 2(0) = 6. Solving for y yields x=2; therefore, an ordered pair for the line is (2, 0). Substituting 0 for x results in 3(0) + 2y = 6. Solving for y yields y=3; therefore, an ordered pair for the line is (0, 3). The two ordered pairs (the x- and y-intercepts) can be plotted and a straight line through them can be constructed.

T - chart

x	y
0	3
2	0

Intercepts

x - intercept: (2, 0)

y - intercept: (0, 3)

3x + 2y = 6

(0,3)

(2,0)

Graphing Linear Equations Exercises

Graph the following linear equations. Also record the slope and y-intercept of each equation.

1   -x + 4y = -16

Slope: _____

y-intercept: _____

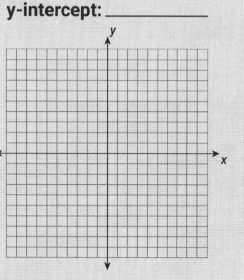

2   3x + y = -4

Slope: _____

y-intercept: _____

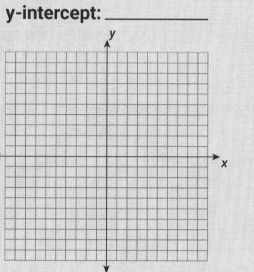

3   5x + 2y = -8

Slope: _____

y-intercept: _____

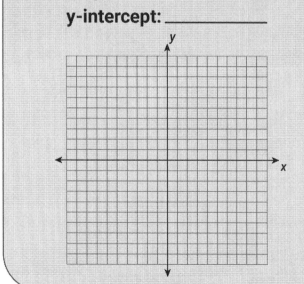

4   -3x + 2y = 6

Slope: _____

y-intercept: _____

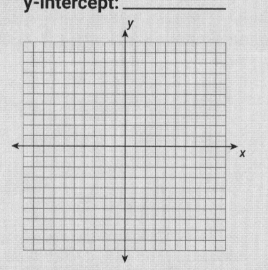

5) $-7x + 3y = 15$

Slope: _____

y-intercept: _____

6) $2x + 3y = -9$

Slope: _____

y-intercept: _____

7) $5x + 6y = -12$

Slope: _____

y-intercept: _____

8) $-x + 2y = 6$

Slope: _____

y-intercept: _____

9 x + y = 3

Slope: _____

y-intercept: _____

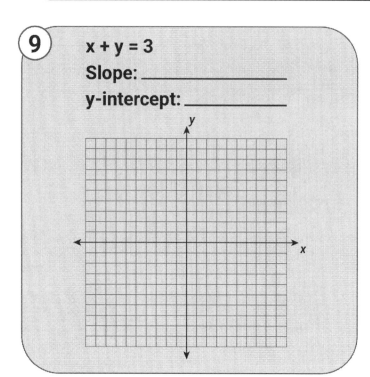

10 -x + 2y = -8

Slope: _____

y-intercept: _____

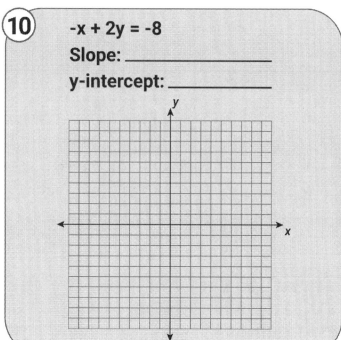

Inequalities

Linear inequalities are a concise mathematical way to express the relationship between unequal values. More specifically, they describe in what way the values are unequal. A value could be greater than (>); less than (<); greater than or equal to (≥); or less than or equal to (≤) another value. The statement "five times a number added to forty is more than sixty-five" can be expressed as $5x + 40 > 65$. Common words and phrases that express inequalities are:

Symbol	Phrase
<	is under, is below, smaller than, beneath
>	is above, is over, bigger than, exceeds
≤	no more than, at most, maximum
≥	no less than, at least, minimum

Solving Linear Inequalities

When solving a linear inequality, the solution is the set of all numbers that makes the statement true. The inequality $x + 2 ≥ 6$ has a solution set of 4 and every number greater than 4 (4.0001, 5, 12, 107, etc.). Adding 2 to 4 or any number greater than 4 would result in a value that is greater than or equal to 6. Therefore, $x ≥ 4$ would be the solution set.

Solution sets for linear inequalities often will be displayed using a number line. If a value is included in the set (≥ or ≤), there is a shaded dot placed on that value and an arrow extending in the direction of the solutions. For a variable > or ≥ a number, the arrow would point right on the number line (the direction where the numbers increase); and if a variable is < or ≤ a number, the arrow would point left (where the numbers decrease). If the value is not included in the set (> or <), an open circle on that value would be used with an arrow in the appropriate direction.

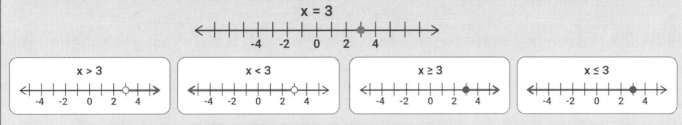

In order to algebraically solve a linear inequality, the same steps should be followed as in solving a linear equation. The inequality symbol stays the same for all operations EXCEPT when dividing by a negative number. If dividing by a negative number while solving an inequality, the relationship reverses (the sign flips). Dividing by a positive does not change the relationship, so the sign stays the same. In other words, > switches to < and vice versa. An example is shown below.

1. Solve $-2(x + 4) ≤ 22$

2. Distribute: $-2x - 8 ≤ 22$

3. Add 8 to both sides: $-2x ≤ 30$

4. Divide both sides by -2 : $x ≥ 15$

Solving Linear Inequalities Exercises

Solve the following inequalities and then graph the solution:

1 $-26 > -3x - 6 + 2x$

2 $48 > 5x - 8 + 2x$

3 $3(6 - 2x) - 4x > 4x - 52$

4 $5x - 146 < 2(3 - 5x) - 4x$

5 $6x - 5 + 3x \geq -77$

6 $4(5 - 3x) < 9x - 64$

7 $2(6 - 2x) \leq 18 - 3(x + 4)$

8 $2(4 - 3x) \geq 8x - 34$

9 $-5(1 - x) > 63 - 3(x + 4)$

10 $8(3 + 2x) - x > -3(x + 4)$

Simplifying Rational Expressions

A rational expression is a ratio or fraction of two polynomials. An expression is in lowest terms when the numerator and denominator have no common factors. The rational expression $\frac{7}{4x + 3}$ is in lowest terms because there are no common factors between the numerator and denominator. The rational expression $\frac{x^2 + 2x + 1}{x^2 - 1}$ can be simplified to $\frac{(x + 1)(x+1)}{(x - 1)(x - 1)} = \frac{x + 1}{x - 1}$ because there is a common factor of x+1.

Simplify the following rational expressions.

1 $\dfrac{8a - 48}{a - 6}$

_____

2 $\dfrac{35}{5a - 45}$

_____

3 $\dfrac{4a - 20}{24}$

_____

4 $\dfrac{a - 2}{a^2 - 11a + 18}$

_____

5 $\dfrac{15a^2}{5a^2}$

_____

6 $\dfrac{a - 7}{a^2 + a - 56}$

_____

7 $\dfrac{18a^3}{15a^3}$

_____

8 $\dfrac{5a + 40}{a + 8}$

_____

9 $\dfrac{40a^4}{16a^4}$

_____

10 $\dfrac{10a^5}{25a^3}$

_____

11 $\dfrac{15a^4}{20a^3}$

_____

12 $\dfrac{a^2 + a - 2}{a - 1}$

_____

13 $\dfrac{a^2 - 11a + 30}{a^2 - 2a - 35}$

_____

14 $\dfrac{a + 7}{a^2 + 13a + 42}$

_____

15 $\dfrac{28a^2 + 42a + 14}{20a^2 - 22a - 16}$

_____

16 $\dfrac{4a^{-1}b^3 - 48}{a - 6}$

_____

17 $(4a^2b^4)^{\frac{3}{2}}$

_____

18 $\dfrac{8a - 48}{a - 6}$

_____

Adding and Subtracting Rational Expressions

In each of the following problems, add or subtract the given rational expressions.
Simplify where possible.

1) $\dfrac{4a^3 - 5b^2}{2a^4} + \dfrac{3a^3 - 3b^2}{2a^4}$

2) $\dfrac{3a^4 - 2b^5}{5a^5b^6} - \dfrac{3a^4 + 7b^5}{5a^5b^6}$

3) $\dfrac{7a^4}{4a^5 - 6} + \dfrac{3a^4 - 8}{4a^5 - 6}$

4) $\dfrac{3a - 7}{5a^4 - 11a} + \dfrac{7a - 5}{5a^4 - 11a}$

5) $\dfrac{5a - 9}{2a^5 + 13a} - \dfrac{3a + 5}{2a^5 + 13a}$

6) $\dfrac{4a^2 + 5b^2}{8a^3} + \dfrac{5a^2 - 6b^2}{8a^3}$

7) $\dfrac{8a - 9b}{6a^3b^2} - \dfrac{8a + 5b}{6a^3b^2}$

8) $\dfrac{a}{7} - \dfrac{4a + 1}{a + 3}$

9) $\dfrac{a}{3} + \dfrac{4a + 5}{a + 4}$

10) $\dfrac{4a}{6} + \dfrac{5a + 8}{3a + 9}$

Solving Rational Equations

Solve each of the following rational equations.

1) $4x - 12 = -2x$

2) $\dfrac{1}{x} = \dfrac{3}{12x} + 6$

3) $\dfrac{x + 11}{18x^2} + \dfrac{10}{9x^2} = \dfrac{x - 4}{9x^2}$

4) $\dfrac{1}{x} = \dfrac{2}{7x} + 11$

5) $\dfrac{1}{x} = \dfrac{12}{10x} + 3$

Factoring Quadratic Equations

Find the solutions to the following quadratic equations by factoring.

1 $x^2 - 9x = -20$

_____

2 $x^2 + 2x = 35$

_____

3 $x^2 - 7x - 18 = 0$

_____

4 $x^2 + 8x = 20$

_____

5 $x^2 + 18x + 77 = 0$

_____

6 $x^2 - 4x - 43 = 2$

_____

7 $x^2 + 5x - 24 = 0$

_____

8 $x^2 + 17x = -72$

_____

9 $6x^2 - 70x - 24 = 0$

_____

10 $x^2 + 22x + 120 = 0$

_____

11 $x^2 - 3x = 88$

_____

12 $x^2 + 11x + 10 = 0$

_____

13 $6x^2 + 8x = 30$

_____

14 $2x^2 - 13x = -15$

_____

15 $4x^2 - 41x = 88$

_____

Solving Quadratic Equations with the Quadratic Formula

The quadratic formula can be used to solve any quadratic equation. This formula may be the longest method for solving quadratic equations and is commonly used as a last resort after other methods are ruled out. It can be helpful in memorizing the formula to see where it comes from, so here are the steps involved.

The most general form for a quadratic equation is $ax^2 + bx + c = 0$.

First, dividing both sides by a leaves us with $x^2 + \dfrac{b}{a}x + \dfrac{c}{a} = 0$.

To complete the square on the left-hand side, c/a can be subtracted on both sides to get $x^2 + \dfrac{b}{a}x = -\dfrac{c}{a}$

$\left(\dfrac{b}{2a}\right)^2$ is then added to both sides.

This gives $x^2 + \dfrac{b}{a}x + \left(\dfrac{b}{2a}\right)^2 = \left(\dfrac{b}{2a}\right)^2 - \dfrac{c}{a}$

The left can now be factored and the right-hand side simplified to give

$$\left(x + \dfrac{b}{2a}\right)^2 = \dfrac{b^2 - 4ac}{4a}$$

Taking the square roots gives $x + \dfrac{b}{2a} = \pm\dfrac{\sqrt{b^2 - 4ac}}{2a}$

Solving for x yields the quadratic formula: $x = \dfrac{-b \pm \sqrt{b^2 - 4ac}}{2a}$

It isn't necessary to remember how to get this formula, but memorizing the formula itself is the goal.

If an equation involves taking a root, then the first step is to move the root to one side of the equation and everything else to the other side. That way, both sides can be raised to the index of the radical in order to remove it, and solving the equation can continue.

Solving Quadratic Equations Exercises

Solve the following quadratic equations using the quadratic formula.

1 $x^2 + 2x - 35 = 0$

2 $x^2 - 5x - 24 = 0$

3 $x^2 + 3x - 54 = 0$

4 $x^2 - 16x + 63 = 0$

5 $x^2 + 3x - 40 = 0$

6 $x^2 - 2x - 120 = 0$

7 $x^2 - 20x - 96 = 0$

8 $x^2 - 9x + 18 = 0$

9 $x^2 - 2x - 24 = 0$

10 $x^2 + 8x + 12 = 0$

11 $x^2 - 13x + 42 = 0$

12 $x^2 - 7x - 60 = 0$

13 $8x^2 - 32x - 40 = 0$

14 $18x^2 + 72x + 72 = 0$

15 $12x^2 - 12x - 72 = 0$

Completing the Square

When an equation has a degree of 2, completing the square is an option. For example, the quadratic equation $x^2 - 6x + 2 = 0$ can be rewritten by completing the square. The goal of completing the square is to get the equation into the form $(x - p)^2 = q$. Using the example, the constant term 2 first needs to be moved over to the opposite side by subtracting. Then, the square can be completed by adding 9 to both sides, which is the square of half of the coefficient of the middle term $-6x$. The current equation is $x^2 - 6x + 9 = 7$. The left side can be factored into a square of a binomial, resulting in $(x - 3)^2 = 7$. To solve for x, the square root of both sides should be taken, resulting in $(x - 3) = \sqrt{\pm 7}$, and $x = 3 \pm \sqrt{7}$.

Solve the following equations in the form of $ax^2 + bx + c = 0$
by completing the square.

1 $x^2 - 2x - 15 = 0$

2 $x^2 + 2x = 35$

3 $x^2 + 2x - 8 = 0$

4 $x^2 + 10x + 7 = -2$

5 $x^2 - 8x - 20 = 0$

6 $x^2 + 18x + 56 = 0$

7 $x^2 - 6x - 55 = 0$

8 $x^2 + 12x - 64 = 0$

9 $x^2 + 8x + 7 = 0$

10 $x^2 - 19x + 90 = 0$

11 $4x^2 - 12x - 4 = 12$

12 $2x^2 - 22x + 60 = 0$

13 $4x^2 + 8x + 22 = 0$

14 $100x^2 - 100x - 9 = 0$

15 $12x^2 - 24x + 6 = -4$

Solving Systems of Equations with Elimination

A system of equations is a group of equations that have the same variables or unknowns. These equations can be linear, but they are not always so. Finding a solution to a system of equations means finding the values of the variables that satisfy each equation. For a linear system of two equations and two variables, there could be a single solution, no solution, or infinitely many solutions.

A single solution occurs when there is one value for x and y that satisfies the system. This would be shown on the graph where the lines cross at exactly one point. When there is no solution, the lines are parallel and do not ever cross. With infinitely many solutions, the equations may look different, but they are the same line. One equation will be a multiple of the other, and on the graph, they lie on top of each other.

The process of elimination can be used to solve a system of equations. For example, the following equations make up a system:

$$x + 3y = 10 \text{ and } 2x - 5y = 9$$

Immediately adding these equations does not eliminate a variable, but it is possible to change the first equation by multiplying the whole equation by -2. This changes the first equation to

$$-2x - 6y = -20$$

The equations can be then added to obtain $-11y = -11$. Solving for y yields $y = 1$. To find the rest of the solution, 1 can be substituted in for y in either original equation to find the value of $x = 7$. The solution to the system is $(7, 1)$ because it makes both equations true, and it is the point in which the lines intersect.

If the system is dependent — having infinitely many solutions — then both variables will cancel out when the elimination method is used, resulting in an equation that is true for many values of x and y.

Since the system is dependent, both equations can be simplified to the same equation or line.

Solving Systems of Equations with Elimination Exercises

Solve the following systems of equations using elimination.

1 $3x + y = -21; x + y = -5$

2 $-5x - 7y = 24; 10x + 7y = 1$

3 $5x - 2y = 18; -2x - y = -9$

4 $x + 3y = 18; -x - 4y = -25$

5 $y = -\frac{3}{2}x - 7; y = \frac{1}{2}x + 5$

6 $y = \frac{1}{4}x - 2; y = -3x - 15$

7 $y = -\frac{2}{7}x - 2; y = -\frac{1}{7}x - 4$

8 $3x + 3y = -3; -3x - 4y = 2$

9 $-x + 2 = y; -6x - 3 = y$

10 $4x - y = -1; -3x + 2y = -3$

Solving Systems of Equations with Substitution

A system can also be solved using substitution. This involves solving one equation for a variable and then plugging that solved equation into the other equation in the system. This equation can be solved for one variable, which can then be plugged in to either original equation to solve for the other variable.

For example, $x - y = -2$ and $3x + 2y = 9$ can be solved using substitution.

The first equation can be solved for x, where $x = -2 + y$.

Then it can be plugged into the other equation:

$$3 - (2 + y) + 2y = 9$$

Solving for y yields:

$$-6 + 3y + 2y = 9$$

That shows that $y = 3$. If $y = 3$, then $x = 1$.

This solution can be checked by plugging in these values for the variables in each equation to see if it makes a true statement.

Solving Systems of Equations with Substitution Exercises

Solve the following systems of equations using substitution.

1 $y = 4x - 10; y = \dfrac{1}{3}x + 1$

2 $y = 4x + 5; y = -\dfrac{1}{3}x - 8$

3 $y = -4x + 15; y = -\dfrac{7}{2}x + 12$

4 $2x - 3y = -1; -x + y = -1$

5 $y = \dfrac{1}{2}x + 4; y = -\dfrac{5}{2}x + 10$

6 $-16 = 8x + y; -3x + y = -5$

7 $5x + 2y = 21; -x - y = -9$

8 $6x - 5y = 12; 2x + y = 20$

9 $5 = 4x - 7y; 9x - 7y = -15$

10 $y = -\dfrac{7}{5}x - 3; y = -\dfrac{4}{9}x - 3$

Using Formulas

Formulas are mathematical expressions that define the value of one quantity given the value of one or more different quantities.

Use your knowledge of evaluating expressions and equations to evaluate the following formulas for the given values.

1 Given the formula d = r × t, what is the value of d when r = 35 mph and t = 6 hours?

_____

_____

2 Given the formula C = $\frac{5}{9}$(F - 32), what is the equivalent Celsius temperature of 80 degrees Fahrenheit?

_____

_____

3 Given the formula P = 2l × 2w, if the total perimeter of a rectangle is 36 cm and the length of each side is 12 cm, what is the width?

_____

_____

4 For a triangle with a base of length b and a height of length h, the area is $\frac{1}{2}$bh. What is the area of a triangle with a height of 6 mm and a base of 12 mm?

_____

_____

5 Given the Pythagorean Theorem, $c^2 = a^2 + b^2$, if the hypotenuse of a triangle, c, is 13 inches and one side is 5 inches, what is the length of the other side?

_____

_____

_____

6 Given that the sum of all internal angles in a polygon equals $180(n - 2)$ degrees, where n is the number of sides, what is the sum of the internal angles on an octagon?

_____

_____

_____

7 The area of a trapezoid can be calculated using the formula: $A = \frac{1}{2} \times h(b_1 + b_2)$, where h is the height and b_1 and b_2 are the parallel bases of the trapezoid. If the area of a given trapezoid is 24 square inches, the height is 4 inches, and one base is 2 inches longer than the other, what are the measurements of both bases?

_____

_____

_____

8 Given the formula for the surface area of a rectangular prism, SA = 2xy + 2yz + 2xz, what is the depth of the prism, z, if the length is 8 inches, the width is 4 inches, and the total surface area is 184 square inches?

_____

_____

9 Given that the volume of a cube is V = s × s × s, and the surface area is SA = 6s², if a cube has a volume of 27 cubic centimeters, what is the surface area?

_____

_____

10 Recall that the sum of all internal angles in a polygon equals 180(n - 2) degrees. The formula for the perimeter of a regular polygon is the number of sides multiplied by the length of one side. The formula for the area (A) of a regular polygon is A= $\frac{1}{2}$ × a × P, where a is the length of the apothem and P is the perimeter of the figure. If a certain regular polygon has internal angles that sum to 540 degrees, an apothem of 6 cm, and an area of 120 square cm, what shape is the polygon and what is the length of one if its sides?

_____

_____

_____

Writing Equations to Model Situations

Write an equation that models each of the following situations.

1 A company invests $50,000 in a building where they can produce saws. The cost of producing one saw is $40. Write an equation that expresses the amount of money the company pays where the variable y is the money paid and x is the number of saws produced and b represents the base cost.

_____

2 The width (w) of a rectangle is 2 centimeters less than the length (l). If the perimeter of the rectangle is 44 centimeters, write an equation that calculates the dimensions of the rectangle.

_____

3 The phone bill is calculated each month based on the amount of data used ($15 per gigabyte, g) plus $20 per line on top of a $10 base fee. Write an equation that would calculate the monthly bill on this plan.

_____

Algebraic Word Problems

Solve each of the following word problems.

1 Carly purchased 84 bulbs for her flower garden. Tulips came in trays containing six bulbs and daffodils came in trays containing 8 bulbs. Carly bought an equal number of tulip and daffodil trays. How many of each type of flower bulb were purchased?

_____

_____

2 Apples cost $2 each, while bananas cost $3 each. Maria purchased 10 fruits in total and spent $22. How many apples did she buy?

_____

_____

3 Jessica buys 10 cans of paint. Red paint costs $1 per can and blue paint costs $2 per can. In total, she spends $16. How many red cans did she buy?

_____

_____

_____

4 Cameron sold half his yo-yo collection then bought six more. He now has 16 yo-yos. How many did he begin with?

_____

_____

_____

5 The sum of three consecutive pages in a book is 144. What is the lowest page number in the set?

_____

_____

6 Jane got 9 tickets from winning a game at the arcade and adds them to her pile. She then spends half of her tickets on a mini football, leaving just 26 left. How many tickets did she have before buying the football?

_____

_____

7 Noah had $165 to spend on 8 identical posters to give as favors at his birthday party. After buying the posters, he had 29 dollars left. How much was each poster?

_____

_____

8 Three-hundred-thirty-one third grade students are taking a field trip to the local science museum. They are filling 7 buses and then 9 students are riding in an accessible van. How many students fit on each bus?

_____

_____

9 After seeing a movie, Dennis, Jan, and Tina decide to split the total cost of the tickets and the snacks. If they each had to pay $13, and the snacks cost $12 total, how much was each ticket?

_____

_____

10 Tiara is selling cups of lemonade for $0.75. If each pitcher makes 8 cups of lemonade and the cost of ingredients is $1.12 per pitcher, how many cups does she need to sell to make $20 profit?

_____

_____

11 Peter and his sister, Lisa, are collecting bottles and cans for redemption and plan to donate the proceeds to the local animal shelter. The redemption center gives $0.05 for each aluminum can, but glass bottles earn $0.10. If they bring their bottles and cans to the redemption center and get $29.00 total after redeeming ¾ as many glass bottles as cans, how many bottles did they redeem?

_____

_____

12 Mei is baking brownies and cookies for a bake sale. The recipe for brownies makes 16 brownies and the recipe for cookies makes 24 cookies. How many batches of cookies does she need to make if she is to bring 184 treats and she makes one more batch of cookies than brownies?

_____

_____

13 Dwayne's baseball team has 44 games on the schedule this season. If ¼ are home games, how many games are away?

_____

_____

14 Juanita is counting ladybugs and spiders that she finds in her backyard. Altogether, she counts 198 legs. If she sees twice as many spiders as ladybugs, how many ladybugs were there?

_____

_____

15 Mr. Read's seventh grade class is studying geography. If he is creating equal-sized groups to present on each of the seven continents and each group has four students, how many students are in the class?

_____

_____

_____

16 Shankar is training for a 10k road race. If he runs 5 miles in 42:30, then how long will it take to run 7 miles if he maintains the same pace?

_____

_____

_____

17 Becca practices piano 7 days a week. Some days, she plays 30 minutes, and some days, she plays 50 minutes in the week. If she played 5 hours and 10 minutes, how many days did she play 50 minutes?

_____

_____

18 Sam's mom works at the local diner. She makes $8 per hour as a base wage plus tips. Last week, she earned $396. If tips made up 1/3 of her pay, how many hours did she work?

_____

_____

19 Valencia babysits a family with 3 kids. She makes $12 per hour. However, when one of the kids had a friend over, she makes an extra $3 per hour. Last month, she babysat 6 times. If one of those times there was an additional child, how much did she make if each occasion was 4 hours (including the one with a friend), except one occasion, which was 6 hours?

_____

_____

20 The soccer team is selling donuts to raise money to buy new uniforms. For every box of donuts that they sell, the team receives $3 towards their new uniforms. There are 15 people on the team. How many boxes does each player need to sell in order to raise $270 for their new uniforms?

_____

_____

21 At the store, Jan spends $90 on apples and oranges. Apples cost $1 each and oranges cost $2 each. If Jan buys the same number of apples as oranges, how many oranges did she buy?

_____

_____

22 Kristen purchases $100 worth of CDs and DVDs. The CDs cost $10 each and the DVDs cost $15. If she bought four DVDs, how many CDs did she buy?

_____

_____

23 In Jim's school, there are 3 girls for every 2 boys. There are 650 students in total. How many students are girls?

_____

_____

24 Kimberley earns $10 an hour babysitting, and after 10 p.m., she earns $12 an hour, with the amount paid being rounded to the nearest hour accordingly. On her last job, she worked from 5:30 p.m. to 11 p.m. In total, how much did Kimberley earn for that job?

_____

_____

25 Store brand coffee beans cost $1.23 per pound. A local coffee bean roaster charges $1.98 per $1\frac{1}{2}$ pounds. How much more would 5 pounds from the local roaster cost than 5 pounds of the store brand?

_____

_____

26 Paint Inc. charges $2000 for painting the first 1,800 feet of trim on a house and $1.00 per foot for each foot after. How much would it cost to paint a house with 3125 feet of trim?

_____

_____

27 Sam is twice as old as his sister, Lisa. Their oldest brother, Ray, will be 25 in three years. If Lisa is 13 years younger than Ray, how old is Sam?

_____

_____

28 A rectangle has a length that is 5 feet longer than three times its width. If the perimeter is 90 feet, what is the length in feet?

_____

_____

Functions

A function is a special kind of relation where, for each value of x, there is only a single value of y that satisfies the relation. So, $x^2 = y^2$ is not a function because in this case, if x is 1, y can be either 1 or -1: the pair (1, 1) and (1, -1) both satisfy the relation. More generally, for this relation, any pair of the form (a, ±a) will satisfy it. On the other hand, consider the following relation: $y = x^2 + 1$. This is a function because for each value of x, there is a unique value of y that satisfies the relation. Notice, however, there are multiple values of x that give us the same value of y. This is perfectly acceptable for a function. Therefore, y is a function of x.

To determine if a relation is a function, check to see if every x-value has a unique corresponding y-value.

The set of all possible values for x in $f(x)$ is called the domain of the function, and the set of all possible outputs is called the range of the function. Note that usually the domain is assumed to be all real numbers, except those for which the expression for $f(x)$ is not defined, unless the problem specifies otherwise. An example of how a function might not be defined is in the case of $f(x) = \frac{1}{x + 1}$, which is not defined when x = -1 (which would require dividing by zero). Therefore, in this case the domain would be all real numbers except x = -1.

Domain and Range

Determine whether each of the following sets of ordered pairs is a function, and find the domain and range.

1 {(7, 2), (6, 6), (-2, 4), (2, 5), (-6, 2)}

Function   Yes   No

Domain: _____

Range: _____

2 {(3, 3), (1, 9), (2, 8), (-7, 4), (6, 7)}

Function   Yes   No

Domain: _____

Range: _____

3 {(4, 8), (5, 1), (2, 6), (-2, -8), (2, -6)}

Function   Yes   No

Domain: _____

Range: _____

4 {(-9, -8), (5, 5), (7, 7), (2, 3), (1, -5)}

Function   Yes   No

Domain: _____

Range: _____

5 {(-3, -5), (2, -8), (8, 5), (-1, -7), (2, -8)}

Function   Yes   No

Domain: _____

Range: _____

6 {(-1, -4), (-3, -6), (-6, -1), (-7, 1), (-9, -3)}

Function   Yes   No

Domain: _____

Range: _____

7 {(-2, 7), (5, -1), (-4, -3), (-2, 2), (3, 6)}

Function   Yes   No

Domain: _____

Range: _____

8 {(-4, 9), (5, 8), (4, -5), (-3, -2), (8, -3)}

Function   Yes   No

Domain: _____

Range: _____

9 {(-9, -2), (-2, -8), (-6, -3), (-2, 0), (2, -3)}

Function   Yes   No

Domain: _____

Range: _____

10 {(-9, -7), (6, -2), (-5, 2), (-9, -8), (-7, -9)}

Function   Yes   No

Domain: _____

Range: _____

11 {(6, 5), (-6, 9), (4, 3), (6, 4), (-7, -8)}

Function   Yes   No

Domain: _____

Range: _____

12 {(7, -1), (8, 5), (1, 5), (7, -1), (-9, 4)}

Function   Yes   No

Domain: _____

Range: _____

13 {(-9, 0), (0, 1), (-8, -9), (-1, -2), (1, -8)}

Function   Yes   No

Domain: _____

Range: _____

14 {(4, 2), (-9, 1), (-3, 0), (-1, 5), (4, -7)}

Function   Yes   No

Domain: _____

Range: _____

15 {(7, 7), (2, -1), (-5, 4), (-6, 6), (-7, 4)}

Function   Yes   No

Domain: _____

Range: _____

16 {(3, 2), (2, 2), (-5, 2), (0, 2), (-2, 2)}

Function   Yes   No

Domain: _____

Range: _____

Complete the Input/Output Table

Use the provided functions to complete the missing values in the input/output tables below.

1 $f(x) = x^2 - 3$

x	f(x)
-2	
	-2
0	
1	
2	

2 $f(x) = 2x + 4$

x	f(x)
-2	
	2
1	
	8
	14

3 $f(x) = 5x^2 - 1$

x	f(x)
	44
-1	
2	
	44
5	

4 $f(x) = 8 - 5x$

x	f(x)
-6	
-3	
0	
	-7
	-17

5 $f(x) = -3x + 6$

x	f(x)
	21
-1	
	6
	-9
	-15

6 $f(x) = x^2 - 2$

x	f(x)
-4	
-3	
0	
1	
2	

7 $f(x) = 3 - 2x$

x	f(x)
	9
	5
	3
	-1
	-5

8 $f(x) = 2x^3$

x	f(x)
-2	
-1	
1	
2	
3	

9 $f(x) = \frac{x}{3}$

x	f(x)
	-2
	-1
	1
	2
	3

10 $f(x) = \frac{x^3}{2}$

x	f(x)
-2	
	0.5
	4
	13.5
	32

Composite Functions

A composite function is one in which two functions are combined such that the output from the first function becomes the input for the second function (one function should be applied after another function). The composition of a function written as $(g \cdot f)(x)$ or $g(f(x))$ is read "g of f of x." The inner function, $f(x)$, would be evaluated first and the answer would be used as the input of the outer function, $g(x)$. To determine the value of a composite function, the value of the inner function should be substituted for the variable of the outer function.

Here's a sample problem:

A store is offering a 20% discount on all of its merchandise. You have a coupon worth $5 off any item. The cost of an item with the 20% discount can be modeled by the function: $d(x) = 0.8x$.

The cost of an item with the coupon can be modeled by the function $c(x) = x-5$. A composition of functions to model the cost of an item applying the discount first and then the coupon would be $c(d(x))$. Replacing $d(x)$ with its value $(0.8x)$ results in $c(0.8x)$. By evaluating the function $c(x)$ with an input of $0.8x$, it is determined that: $c(d(x))=0.8x-5$

To model the cost of an item if the coupon is applied first and then the discount, $d(c(x))$ should be determined. The result would be:
$$d(c(x))=0.8x-4$$

Work through the following composite functions to find the requested value.

1 If $g(x) = x^3 - 3x^2 - 2x + 6$ and $f(x) = 2$, then what is $g(f(x))$?

2 If $g(x) = x - 8$ and $f(x) = x + 2$, then what is $g(f(x))$?

3 If g(x) = x - 5 and f(x) = x - 7, then what is g(f(x))?

_____

_____

_____

4 If g(x) = 5x + 3 and f(x) = -x + 1, then what is g(f(x))?

_____

_____

_____

5 If g(x) = x + 3 and f(x) = x - 2, then what is g(f(x))?

_____

_____

_____

6 If g(x) = 2x + 8 and f(x) = 5x + 1, then what is g(f(x))?

_____

_____

_____

7 If g(x) = x - 3 and f(x) = 2x + 1, then what is g(f(x))?

_____

_____

_____

8 If g(x) = 2x - 1 and ƒ(x) = x - 9, then what is g(ƒ(x))?

_____

_____

_____

9 If g(x) = 3x + 1 and ƒ(x) = 3x - 8, then what is g(ƒ(x))?

_____

_____

_____

10 If g(x) = 3 - 2x and ƒ(x) = x + 6, then what is g(ƒ(x))?

_____

_____

_____

11 If g(x) = 2 + 9x and ƒ(x) = 3 - x, then what is g(ƒ(x))?

_____

_____

_____

12 If h(x) = x - 2, g(x) = x + 1 and ƒ(x) = x - 3, then what is h(g(ƒ(x)))?

_____

_____

_____

13 If h(x) = x - 6, g(x) = x - 3 and f(x) = x - 9, then what is h(g(f(x)))?

_____

_____

_____

14 If h(x) = x + 3, g(x) = 5x - 9 and f(x) = x - 8, then what is h(g(f(x)))?

_____

_____

_____

15 If h(x) = 2x - 4, g(x) = x + 7 and f(x) = x - 5, then what is h(g(f(x)))?

_____

_____

_____

16 If h(x) = 3x - 7, g(x) = -4x + 1 and f(x) = 6x + 9, then what is h(g(f(x)))?

_____

_____

_____

17 If h(x) = 12x + 3, g(x) = x - 4 and f(x) = 3x, then what is h(g(f(x)))?

_____

_____

_____

18 If $h(x) = 2x - 4$, $g(x) = 4x - 1$ and $f(x) = 5 + x$, then what is $h(g(f(x)))$?

19 If $h(x) = 2x + 1$, $g(x) = 4 + 7x$ and $f(x) = 9x - 3$, then what is $h(g(f(x)))$?

20 If $h(x) = 7x - 4$, $g(x) = 3x + 8$ and $f(x) = 2 + x$, then what is $h(g(f(x)))$?

Putting It All Together

The following multiple-choice questions will test your ability to synthesize all of the algebra concepts you have mastered. Review each question and circle the correct answer.

1 What is the slope of this line?

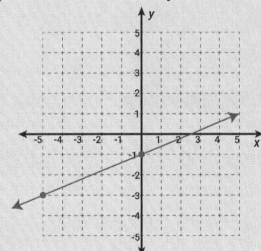

a. 2

b. $\dfrac{5}{2}$

c. $\dfrac{1}{2}$

d. $\dfrac{2}{5}$

_____
_____
_____
_____
_____
_____
_____

2 The variable y is directly proportional to x. If y = 3 when x = 5, then what is y when x = 20?

a. 10 _____

b. 12 _____

c. 14 _____

d. 16 _____

3 A line passes through the point (1, 2) and crosses the y-axis at y = 1. Which of the following is an equation for this line?

a. y = 2x _____

b. y = x + 1 _____

c. x + y = 1 _____

d. $y = \dfrac{x}{2} - 2$ _____

4 There are 4x+1 treats in each party favor bag. If a total of 60x + 15 treats are distributed, how many bags are given out?

a. 15 _____

b. 16 _____

c. 20 _____

d. 22 _____

5 What is the value of the expression: $7^2 - 3 \times (4 + 2) + 15 \div 5$?

a. 12.2 _____

b. 40.2 _____

c. 34 _____

d. 58.2 _____

6 What are the roots of $x^2 + x - 2$?

a. 1 and -2 _____

b. -1 and 2 _____

c. 2 and -2 _____

d. 9 and 13 _____

7 What is the y-intercept of $y = x^{5/3} + (x - 3)(x + 1)$?

a. 3.5 _____

b. 7.6 _____

c. -3 _____

d. -15.1 _____

8 $x^4 - 16$ can be simplified to which of the following?

a. $(x^2 - 4)(x^2 + 4)$ _____

b. $(x^2 + 4)(x^2 + 4)$ _____

c. $(x^2 - 4)(x^2 - 4)$ _____

d. $(x^2 - 2)(x^2 + 4)$ _____

9 If $3x = 6y = -2z = 24$, then what does $4xy + z$ equal?

a. 116 _____

b. 130 _____

c. 84 _____

d. 108 _____

10 If $\dfrac{5}{2} \div \dfrac{1}{3} = n$ then n is between:

a. 5 and 7 _____

b. 7 and 9 _____

c. 9 and 11 _____

d. 3 and 5 _____

11 Which inequality represents the following number line?

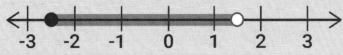

a. $-\dfrac{5}{2} \leq x < \dfrac{3}{2}$ _____

b. $-\dfrac{7}{2} \leq x < \dfrac{5}{2}$ _____

c. $-\dfrac{5}{2} < x \leq \dfrac{3}{2}$ _____

d. $\dfrac{5}{2} < x \leq -\dfrac{3}{2}$ _____

12 Which of the following inequalities is equivalent to $3 - \frac{1}{2}x \geq 2$?

a. $x \geq 2$

b. $x \leq 2$

c. $x \geq 1$

d. $x \leq 1$

13 A line passes through the origin and through the point $(-3, 4)$. What is the slope of the line?

a. $-\frac{4}{3}$

b. $-\frac{3}{4}$

c. $\frac{4}{3}$

d. $\frac{3}{4}$

14 The expression $\frac{x - 4}{x^2 - 6x + 8}$ is undefined for what value(s) of x?

a. 4 and 2

b. -4 and -2

c. 2

d. 4

15 Of the given sets of coordinates below, which one lies on the line that is perpendicular to $y = 2x - 3$ and passes through the point $(0, 5)$?

a. $(2, 4)$

b. $(-2, 7)$

c. $(4, -3)$

d. $(-6, 10)$

16 Which of the following is a factor of both $x^2 + 4x + 4$ and $x^2 - x - 6$?

    a. x - 3

    b. x + 2

    c. x - 2

    d. x + 3

17 17. What is the solution to the following system of equations?
$x^2 - 2x + y = 8$, $x - y = -2$

    a. (-2, 3)

    b. There is no solution

    c. (-2, 0), (1, 3)

    d. (-2, 0), (3, 5)

18 What are the y-intercept(s) for $y = x^2 + 3x - 4$?

    a. y = 1

    b. y = -4

    c. y = 3

    d. y = 4

19 What would the equation be for the following problem?
3 times the sum of a number and 7 is greater than or equal to 32

    a. 3(7n) > 32

    b. $3 \times n + 7 \geq 32$

    c. 3n + 21 > 32

    d. $3(n + 7) \geq 32$

20 Which inequality represents the following number line?

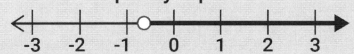

-3   -2   -1   0   1   2   3

a. $4x + 5 < 8$ _____

b. $-4x + 5 < 8$ _____
_____

c. $-4x + 5 > 8$ _____

d. $4x - 5 > 8$ _____

21 What is the slope of the line that passes through the points (10, -4) and (-5, 8)?

a. $-\frac{5}{4}$ _____

b. $-\frac{4}{15}$ _____

c. $-\frac{4}{5}$ _____

d. $-\frac{12}{5}$ _____

22 What is the solution to the following system of equations?
$x^2 + y = 4, \ 2x + y = 1$

a. (-1, 3) _____

b. (-1, 3), (3, -5) _____

c. (3, -5) _____

d. -1, 3 _____

23 If $f(x) = x^2 - 3x + 17$, then what is $f(x + 1)$?

a. $x^2 - 3x + 19$ _____

b. $x^2 - x + 15$ _____

c. $x^2 + 2x + 18$ _____

d. $x^2 - 3x + 14$ _____

ANSWER EXPLANATIONS

Order of Operations

(1) **13**: The problem was $4 + (3 \times 2)^2 \div 4$. First, the operation within the parentheses must be completed, yielding: $4 + 6^2 \div 4$. Second, the exponent is evaluated: $4 + 36 \div 4$. Third, the division is conducted: $4 + 9$. Fourth, addition is completed, giving the answer: 13.

(2) **2**: $2 \times (6 + 3) \div (2 + 1)^2$. The first step is to complete the operations in parentheses. $2 \times 9 \div (3)^2$. Then exponents: $2 \times 9 \div 9$. Then multiplication: $18 \div 9$. Then divide: 2.

(3) **7**: For $2^2 \times (3 - 1) \div 2 + 3$, the operations in the parentheses must be completed first: $2^2 \times 2 \div 2 + 3$. Exponents: $4 \times 2 \div 2 + 3$. Multiply: $8 \div 2 + 3$. Divide: $4 + 3$. Add: 7.

(4) **65**: $(12 + 3) \times (8 - 2) - 5^2$; $15 \times 6 - 5^2$; $15 \times 6 - 25$; $90 - 25 = 65$.

(5) **114**: $(19 - 8) \times (13 - 3) + 2^2$; $11 \times 10 + 2^2$; $11 \times 10 + 4$; $110 + 4 = 114$.

(6) **48**: $(2 + 4)^2 + (9 + 12 \div 4)$; $(6)^2 + (9 + 3)$; $36 + 12 = 48$

(7) **297**: $3 \times (13 \times 3 + 8)^2 - 12$; $3 \times (13 \times 3 + 64) - 12$; $3 \times (103) - 12$; $309 - 12 = 297$

(8) **53**: $[(4 + 3)^2 + 1] + 2^3 - 5$; $(7^2 + 1) + 2^3 - 5$; $50 + 8 - 5 = 53$

(9) **8**: $[6^2 + (20 \div 5 + 4^2)] \div 7$; $[6^2 + (20 \div 5 + 16)] \div 7$; $[6^2 + (4 + 16)] \div 7$; $6^2 + 20 \div 7$; $(36 + 20) \div 7$; $56 \div 7 = 8$.

(10) **-14**: $(155)^2 - [(12 + 2) + 3^2]$; $(3)^2 - (14 + 3^2)$; $9 - 14 + 9$; $9 - 23 = -14$

ANSWER EXPLANATIONS

Translating Algebraic Expressions

1 $9k - 5$

2 $4b + 12$

3 $a^2 + 7d$

4 $(3p - 9) \div 2$

5 $2 \times (8 + r)$

6 $\frac{3}{5} z \times (y - 1)$

7 $4x - 14y^2$

8 $(\frac{1}{5} g + \frac{2}{3} m) - 2$

9 $\frac{1}{2} g + (10 \div a)$

10 $d \times (v - 2)) + 15$

Evaluating Algebraic Expressions

1 **10**: Each instance of x is replaced with 2, and each instance of y is replaced with 3 to get $2^2 - 2 \times 2 \times 3 + 2 \times 3^2 = 4 - 12 + 18 = 10$

2 **608**: Each instance of n is replaced with 4 to get:
$$8n + 5n^3 + 16n^2$$
$$= 8(4) + 5(4)^3 + 16(4)^2$$
$$= 32 + 320 + 256$$
$$= 608$$

3 **-2028**: Each instance of t is replaced with -2, and each instance of g is replaced with 7 to get:
$$(15 - 8t^2) - (5g^3 - 9 + 6g^2) + (3 + 7t)$$
$$= (15 - 8(-2)^2) - (5(7)^3 - 9 + 6(7)^2) + (3 + 7(-2))$$
$$= (15 - 32) - (1715 - 9 + 294) + (3 - 14)$$
$$= (-17) - (2000) + (-11)$$
$$= -2028$$

ANSWER EXPLANATIONS

Evaluating Algebraic Expressions

(4) **-180,072**: Each instance of t is replaced with 3, and each instance of b is replaced with -6 to get

$$(2a^2 + 6a^4 - 4a)(3b^3 + 8b^2 + b)$$
$$= (2(3)^2 + 6(3)^4 - 4(3)) (3(-6)^3 + 8(-6)^2 + (-6))$$
$$= (18 + 486 - 12) (-648 + 288 - 6)$$
$$= (492) (-366)$$
$$= -180,072$$

(5) **1008**: Each instance of k is replaced with 12, and each instance of l is replaced with -8 to get

$$9k^2 - 6l^2 + 8k$$
$$= 9(12)^2 - 6(-8)^2 + 8(12)$$
$$= 1296 - 384 + 96$$
$$= 1,008$$

(6) **21**: Each instance of b is replaced with 2 to get

$$(8b^2 + 3) + (58 - 2b^3) - (6b^3 + 4b)$$
$$= (8(2)^2 + 3) + (58 - 2(2)^3) - (6(2)^3 + 4(2))$$
$$= (32 + 3) + (58 - 16) - (48 + 8)$$
$$= (35) + (42) - (56)$$
$$= 21$$

(7) **-411**: Each instance of c is replaced with -4, and each instance of d is replaced with 3 to get

$$(8c^3 - 6c^2 + 4) + (3d^3 + 7c^2)$$
$$= (8(-4)^3 - 6(-4)^2 + 4) + 3(3)^3 + 7(-4)^2)$$
$$= (-512 - 384 + 4) + (27 + 63)$$
$$= (-892) + (90)$$
$$= -411$$

ANSWER EXPLANATIONS

Evaluating Algebraic Expressions

(8) **-3948**: Each instance of x is replaced with -3, and each instance of y is replaced with 7 to get

$$y(9 - 7x^4 + 2x)$$
$$= 7(9 - 7(-3)^4 + 2(-3))$$
$$= 7(9 - 567 - 6)$$
$$= 7(-564)$$
$$= -3,948$$

(9) **828**: Each instance of c is replaced with 14, and each instance of d is replaced with 4 to get

$$(8 + 4c^2) - (2d^3 - 3d^2)$$
$$= (8 + 4(15)^2) - (2(4)^3 - 3(4)^2)$$
$$= (908) - (128 - 48)$$
$$= 828$$

(10) **55**: Each instance of m is replaced with 1, and each instance of n is replaced with -1 to get

$$(2m^2 + 3)(4n^2 - 7n)$$
$$= (2(1)^2 + 3)(4(-1)^2 - 7(-1))$$
$$= (5)(11)$$
$$= 55$$

ANSWER EXPLANATIONS

Solving Equations

1 Add 3 to both sides to get 4x = 8. Then divide both sides by 4 to get x = 2.

2 First, subtract 4 from each side. This yields 6x = 12. Now, divide both sides by 6 to obtain x = 2.

3 Start by squaring both sides to get 1 + x = 16. Then subtract 1 from both sides to get x = 15.

4 Multiply both sides by x to get x + 2 = 2x, which simplifies to -x = -2, or x = 2.

5 The first step in solving this equation is to collect like terms on the left side of the equation. This yields the new equation -4 + 8x = 8 - 10x. The next step is to move the x-terms to one side by adding 10 to both sides, making the equation -4 + 18x = 8. Then the -4 can be moved to the right side of the equation to form 18x = 12. Dividing both sides of the equation by 18 gives a value of 0.67, or $\frac{2}{3}$.

6 x = 150.

Set up the initial equation:
$\frac{2x}{5} - 1 = 59$
Add 1 to both sides:
$\frac{2x}{5} - 1 + 1 = 59 + 1$
Multiply both sides by 5/2:
$\frac{2x}{5} \times \frac{5}{2} = 60 \times \frac{5}{2} = 150$
x = 150

7
25 = 5(3 + x)
25 = 15 + 5x
10 = 5x; x = 2

8
12 = 2(3x + 4)
12 = 6x + 8
4 = 6x; x = $\frac{2}{3}$

9
8 = 5(3 + 6x)
8 = 15 + 30x
-7 = 30x
x = $\frac{-7}{30}$

10
8 + 5x = 3(2 - 9x)
8 + 5x = 6 - 27x
2 = -32x; x = $-\frac{1}{16}$

11
-6 = 10(4x + 3)
-6 = 40x + 30
-36 = 40x; x = $-\frac{9}{10}$

12
2 - 6x = 3 + 4(5 - 9x)
2 - 6x = 3 + 20 - 36x
30x = 21; x = $\frac{7}{10}$

13
10 - 9x = 3 + 4(6 - 2x)
10 - 9x = 3 + 24 - 8x
x = -17

14
4x = 7(2x + 10)
4x = 14x + 70
10x = -70; x = -7

15
12 = 2(x² - 11) + 2
12 = 2x² - 22 + 2
32 = 2x²
16 = x²; x = 4

16
3(15 - 2x) = (x - 3)²
45 - 6x = x² - 6x + 9
45 = x² + 9
36 = x²; x = 6

ANSWER EXPLANATIONS

Solving Equations

17 First, subtract 9 from both sides to isolate the radical. Then, cube each side of the equation to obtain 2x + 11 = 27. Subtract 11 from both sides, and then divide by 2. The result is x = 8. Plug 8 back into the original equation to obtain the true statement to check the answer:

$$\sqrt[3]{16 + 11} + 9$$
$$\sqrt[3]{27} + 9$$
$$3 + 9 = 12$$

18 The equation can be solved by factoring the numerator into (x + 6)(x - 5). Since that same factor (x - 5) exists on top and bottom, that factor cancels. This leaves the equation x + 6 = 11. Solving the equation gives the answer x = 5. When this value is plugged into the equation, it yields a zero in the denominator of the fraction. Since this is undefined, there is no solution.

Adding and Subtracting Polynomials

1 $(x^3 - 3x^2 + 2x - 2) - (3x^3 + 4x - 3) = -2x^3 - 3x^2 - 2x + 1$

The implied +1 in front of the first set of parentheses will not change those four terms; however, distributing the implied -1 in front of the second set of parentheses will change the sign of each of those three terms:

$$x^3 - 3x^2 + 2x - 2 - 3x^3 - 4x + 3$$

Combining like terms yields:

$$-2x^3 - 3x^2 - 2x + 1$$

2 $3x^2 - 3x + 11$. By distributing the implied one in front of the first set of parentheses and the − 1 in front of the second set of parentheses, the parentheses can be eliminated:

$$1(5x^2 - 3x + 4) - 1(2x^2 - 7) = 5x^2 - 3x + 4 - 2x^2 + 7$$

Next, like terms (same variables with same exponents) are combined by adding the coefficients and keeping the variables and their powers the same:

$$5x^2 - 3x + 4 - 2x^2 + 7 = 3x^2 - 3x + 11$$

ANSWER EXPLANATIONS

Adding and Subtracting Polynomials

3 $(7n + 3n^3 + 3) + (8n + 5n^3 + 2n^4) = 2n^4 + 8n^3 + 15n + 3$

4 $(9 - 7x^4) - (2x^4 + 3) = -9x^4 + 6$

5 $(8 + 4d^2) - (2d^3 - 6 - 3d^2) = -2d^3 + 7d^2 + 14$

6 $(2m^2 + 3) - (4m^2 - 7 + m^4) = -m^4 - 2m^2 + 10$

7 $(4 - 8t^2) - (5t^3 - 9 + 6t^2) + (3 + 7t) = -5t^3 - 14t^2 + 7t + 16$

8 $(2a^2 + 6a^4 - 4a) - (3a^2 + 8a^3 + a) + (7a^3 - 5a^4 - 9a^2) = a^4 - a^3 - 10a^2 - 5a$

9 $(2k - 5k^4) + (7k + 4k^3) - (9k^3 - 6k^4 + 8k) = k^4 - 5k^3 + k$

10 $(8b^5 + 3) + (5b^5 + 8 - 2b^3) - (6b^3 + 4b) = 13b^5 - 8b^3 - 4b + 11$

11 $(2 - 9c^3 + 5c^4) - (8c^4 - 6c^2 + 4) - (3c^3 + 7c^2) = -3c^4 - 12c^3 - c^2 - 2$

12 $(5a^2 - 7a + 2) - (8a - 9) + (4c^4 + 6a + 3) = 4a^4 + 11a^2 - 15a + 14$

ANSWER EXPLANATIONS

Multiplying Monomials and Polynomials

1 $6(3r - 4) = 18r - 24$

2 $12(3x^2 + x) = 36x^2 + 12x$

3 $y^2(y + 15) = y^3 + 15y^2$

4 $5x(x + 4) = 5x^2 + 20x$

5 $2(7x^2 + 3x - 8) = 14x^2 + 6x - 16$

6 $4x^2(-x + 3) = -4x^3 + 12x$

7 $6x(7x^2 - 3x + 1) = 42x^3 - 18x^2 + 6x$

8 The solution for this is: $5x^5 + 13x^4 - 9x^3 + 11x^2 + 7x - 3$. The general principle of distributing each term can be applied when multiplying polynomials of any size. To multiply $(x^2 + 3x - 1)(5x^3 - 2x^2 + 2x + 3)$, all three terms should be distributed from the first polynomial to each of the four terms in the second polynomial and then any like terms should be combined.

$$(5x^5 - 2x^4 + 2x^3 + 3x^2) + (15x^4 - 6x^3 + 6x^2 + 9x) + (-5x^3 + 2x^2 - 2x - 3)$$

$$5x^5 - 2x^4 + 15x^4 + 2x^3 - 6x^3 - 5x^3 + 3x^2 + 2x^2 + 6x^2 + 9x - 2x - 3$$

The final answer should equal:
$$5x^5 + 13x^4 - 9x^3 + 11x^2 + 7x - 3$$

9 $(x + 2)(x - 3)(x - 3) = x^3 - 4x^2 - 3x + 18$

10 $2x^2(7x^2 - 9x + 2) = 14x^4 - 18x^3 + 4x^2$

11 $3x(x^2 + xy + 4y^2) = 3x^3 + 3x^2y + 12xy^2$

12 $6x^3(3x^2 + 2xy + 5y^2) = 18x^5 + 12x^4y + 30x^3y^2$

13 $(4x + 2)^2 = 16x^2 + 16x + 4$

14 $(x + 4)^2 = x^2 + 8x + 16$

15 $(x - 5)(x + 5) = x^2 - 25$

16 $(6x - 9)(6x - 9) = 36x^2 - 108x + 81$

17 $(8x + 3)^2 = 64x^2 + 48x + 9$

ANSWER EXPLANATIONS

Multiplying Monomials and Polynomials

18 $(x+2)(x^2 + 5x - 6) = x^3 + 7x^2 + 4x - 12$. Finding the product means distributing one polynomial to the other so that each term in the first is multiplied by each term in the second. Then, like terms can be collected.
Multiplying the factors yields the expression:
$$x^3 + 5x^2 - 6x + 2x^2 + 10x - 12$$
Collecting like terms means adding the x^2 terms and adding the x terms. The final answer after simplifying the expression is:
$$x^3 + 7x^2 + 4x - 12$$

Multiplying Polynomials Using the FOIL Method

1
$$(x \times x) \quad + \quad (x \times 4) \quad + \quad (10 \times x) \quad + \quad (10 \times 4)$$
First   Outer   Inner   Last
After multiplying these binomials, it's time to solve the operations and combine like terms. Thus, the expression becomes: $x^2 + 4x + 10x + 40 = x^2 + 14x + 40$

2 $(x - 2)(x + 8) = x^2 + 8x +- 2x +- 16 = x^2 + 6x - 16$

3 $(x - 3)(x + 12) = x^2 + 12x +- 3x +- 36 = x^2 + 9x - 36$

4 $(x + 15)(x - 1) = x^2 +- x + 15x +- 15 = x^2 + 14x - 15$

5 $(x + 10)(x + 6) = x^2 + 6x + 10x + 60 = x^2 + 16x + 60$

6 $(x - 4)(x + 9) = x^2 + 9x +- 4x +- 36 = x^2 + 5x - 36$

7 $(x - 7)(x - 5) = x^2 +- 5x +- 7x + 35 = x^2 - 12x + 35$

8 $(x + 8)(x + 1) = x^2 + x + 8x + 8 = x^2 + 9x + 8$

9 $(x + 6)(x + 3) = x^2 + 3x + 6x + 18 = x^2 + 9x + 18$

10 $(x - 10)(x - 2) = x^2 +- 2x +- 10x + 20 = x^2 - 12x + 20$

ANSWER EXPLANATIONS

Factoring

1 $(b^2 - 5b) = b(b - 5)$

2 $(x^2 - 16) = (x - 4)(x + 4)$

3 $(t^2 + 4t) = t(t + 4)$

4 $k^2 - k - 56 = (k + 7)(k - 8)$

5 $t^2 + 11t + 18 = (t + 9)(t + 2)$

6 $(5a^2 + 5a) = 5a(a + 1)$

7 $(t^2 - 3t) = t(t - 3)$

8 $a^2 + 7a + 12 = (a + 4)(a + 3)$

9 $3w^2 - 12w - 135 = 3(w - 9)(w + 5)$

10 $(a^2 - 9) = (a + 3)(a - 3)$

11 $5p^2 + 5p - 150 = 5(p + 6)(p - 5)$

12 $40c^2 - 36c - 36 = 4(5c + 3)(2c - 3)$

13 $(100y^2 - 36) = (10y - 6)(10y + 6)$

14 $3g^2 + 12g - 36 = 3(g - 2)(g + 6)$

15 $(25x^2 - 64) = (5x - 8)(5x + 8)$

16 $16y^2 - 60y + 56 = 4(y - 2)(4y - 7)$

17 $6r^2 + 31r + 40 = (3r + 8)(2r + 5)$

18 $30v^2 - 105v - 135 = 15(v + 1)(2v - 9)$

19 $6d^2 + 2d - 28 = 2(d - 2)(3d + 7)$

20 $24f^2 + 12f - 36 = 12(f - 1)(2f + 3)$

Finding Zeros of Polynomials

1 $x = \frac{2}{3}$, 3: The given equation, $y = (3x - 2)(x - 3)$, is already in factored form, so to find the zeros, each factor just needs to be set equal to zero and solved.

Therefore,

$(3x - 2) = 0$

$3x = 2; x = \frac{2}{3}$

And:

$(x - 3) = 0$

$x = 3$

Thus, the equation has zeros, or x-intercepts, at $\frac{2}{3}$ and 3.

ANSWER EXPLANATIONS

Finding Zeros of Polynomials

(2) $x = \frac{5}{3}$, -5: The given equation, $y = (3x - 5)(x + 5)$, is already in factored form, so to find the zeros, each factor just needs to be set equal to zero and solved.

Therefore,

$(3x - 5) = 0$

$3x = 5; x = \frac{5}{3}$

And:

$(x + 5) = 0$

$x = -5$

Thus, the equation has zeros, or x-intercepts, at $\frac{5}{3}$ and -5.

(3) $x = \frac{4}{5}$ and 7: To find the zeros, the equation, $y = 5x^2 - 39x + 28$, first needs to be factored:

$y = (5x - 4)(x - 7)$

Then, each factor is set equal to zero to solve for x:

$0 = (5x - 4)$

$4 = 5x; x = \frac{4}{5}$

And:

$(x - 7) = 0; x = 7$

So the x-intercepts are at $\frac{4}{5}$ and 7.

(4) $x = 0$, -2: This particular equation can be factored into:

$y = x(x^2 + 4x + 4)$

$x(x + 2)(x + 2)$

By setting each factor equal to zero and solving for x, there are two solutions, $x = 0$, -2. On a graph, these zeros can be seen where the line crosses the x-axis.

(5) $x = 4$, -5: $y = (x^2 + x - 20)$ can be factored into:

$y = (x - 4)(x + 5)$

Then, setting each factor equal to zero yields the x-intercepts of 4 and -5.

ANSWER EXPLANATIONS

Finding Zeros of Polynomials

6 $x = 0, -1, 4$: Again, finding the zeros for a function by factoring is done by setting the equation equal to zero, then completely factoring. Since there was a common x for each term in the provided equation, that is factored out first. Then the quadratic that is left can be factored into two binomials: $(x + 1)(x - 4)$. Setting each factor equation equal to zero and solving for x yields three zeros. $0 = x(x + 1)(x - 4)$; $x = 0, -1, 4$.

7 $\frac{4}{5}$ and $-\frac{3}{4}$: The polynomial $y = (20x^2 - x - 12)$ factors into:
$$y = (4x + 3)(5x - 4)$$
Setting each factor equal to zero and then solving for x gives us our x-intercepts:
$$0 = (4x + 3)$$
$$-3 = 4x; x = -\frac{3}{4}$$
And:
$$0 = (5x - 4)$$
$$4 = 5x; x = \frac{4}{5}$$

8 $x = \frac{2}{5}, -\frac{3}{5}$: The polynomial $y = (10x^2 - 19x - 15)$ factors into:
$$y = (5x + 3)(2x - 5)$$
Setting each factor equal to zero and then solving for x gives us our x-intercepts:
$$0 = (5x + 3)$$
$$-3 = 5x; x = -\frac{3}{5}$$
And:
$$0 = (2x - 5)$$
$$5 = 2x; x = \frac{2}{5}$$

9 $x = 2, -4, -3$: We need to factor the polynomial $y = (x^3 + 5x^2 - 2x - 24)$ into $(x - 2)(x + 4)(x + 3)$. From there, we can set each factor equal to zero and solve for x, yielding three roots: $x = 2, -4, -3$.

ANSWER EXPLANATIONS

Finding Zeros of Polynomials

(10) $x = -2, -3, 3$: It takes a few steps to factor the polynomial $y = (x^2 + 2x - 8)$.
First, we will group it into:
$$y = (x^3 + 2x^2) + (-9x - 18)$$
Then, we will factor each group:
$$y = x^2(x + 2) + -9(x + 2)$$
$$= (x^2 - 9)(x - 2)$$
Then, we can use the difference of squares formula to factor the first factor further, yielding:
$$y = (x - 3)(x + 3)(x + 2)$$
Setting each factor equal to zero and then solving for x gives us our x-intercepts: $x = -2, -3, 3$.

(11) $x = 3, 4$: The polynomial $y = (x^2 - 7x + 12)$ factors into:
$$y = (x - 3)(x - 4)$$
From there, we can set each factor equal to zero and solve for x, which allows us to determine the roots to be $x = 3, 4$.

(12) $x = \dfrac{2}{5}, \dfrac{4}{5}$: The polynomial $y = (25x^2 - 30x + 8)$ factors into:
$$y = (5x - 2)(5x - 4)$$
Setting each factor equal to zero and solving for x yields:
$$0 = (5x - 2)$$
$$2 = 5x;\ x = \frac{2}{5}$$
And:
$$0 = (5x - 4)$$
$$4 = 5x;\ x = \frac{4}{5}$$
So, the zeros of the equation are $x = \dfrac{2}{5}, \dfrac{4}{5}$.

(13) $x = \dfrac{3}{4}, \dfrac{4}{3}$: The polynomial $y = (12x^2 - 25x + 12)$ factors into $y = (4x - 3)(3x - 4)$.
Then, we set each factor equal to zero and solve for x to find the roots:
$$0 = (4x - 3)$$
$$3 = 4x;\ x = \frac{3}{4}$$
And:
$$0 = (3x - 4)$$
$$4 = 3x;\ x = \frac{4}{3}$$
Therefore, our two roots are $x = \dfrac{3}{4}, \dfrac{4}{3}$.

ANSWER EXPLANATIONS

Finding Zeros of Polynomials

14 $x = -3, -5, -4$: The polynomial $y = (x^3 + 12x^2 + 47x + 60)$ factors into:
$$y = (x + 3)(x + 5)(x + 4)$$
Therefore, after setting each factor equal to zero, we can determine the roots to be $x = -3, -5, -4$.

15 $x = -\frac{4}{5}, \frac{2}{5}$: The polynomial $y = (25x^2 + 10x - 8)$ factors into $y = (5x + 4)(5x - 2)$. Then, we need to set each factor equal to zero and solve for x:
$$0 = (5x - 2)$$
$$2 = 5x; x = \frac{2}{5}$$
And:
$$0 = (5x + 4)$$
$$-4 = 5x; x = -\frac{4}{5}$$
Therefore, our roots are $x = -\frac{4}{5}, \frac{2}{5}$.

Finding Slope from Coordinate Pairs

1 slope = 1

2 slope = 2/3

3 slope = 2

4 slope = -6

5 slope = 10

6 slope = 1

7 slope = 2/3

8 slope = -1/3

9 slope = 1/10

10 slope = 5

Finding Linear Equations from Graphs

1 $y = -6x - 3$

2 $y = -x + 4$

3 $y = -\frac{4}{3}x - 1$

4 $y = 2x - 4$

5 $y = 6x - 3$

6 $y = -3x - 3$

7 $y = \frac{3}{2} + 3$

8 $y = -x + 4$

9 $y = \frac{7}{3}x + 5$

10 $y = -\frac{2}{3} - 2$

11 $y = \frac{1}{2}x - 1$

12 $y = 2x - 2$

13 $y = \frac{1}{2}x - 1$

14 $y = -\frac{7}{3}x + 4$

15 $y = 2x + 4$

16 $y = -\frac{4}{3}x - 1$

17 $y = -6x + 3$

18 $y = 4x - 4$

19 $y = \frac{1}{2}x - 1$

20 $y = \frac{7}{4}x - 3$

ANSWER EXPLANATIONS

Graphing Linear Equations

1 Slope: ¼   y-intercept: -4

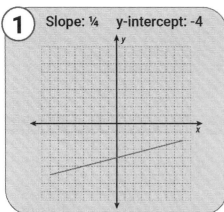

2 Slope: -3   y-intercept: -4

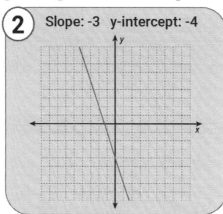

3 Slope: -5/2 y-intercept: -4

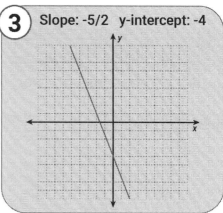

4 Slope: 3/2   y-intercept: 3

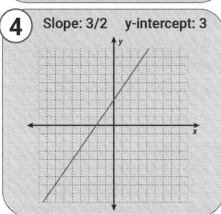

5 Slope: 7/3   y-intercept: 5

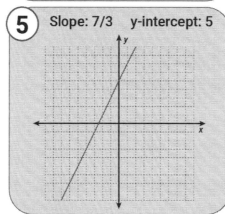

6 Slope: -2/3   y-intercept: -3

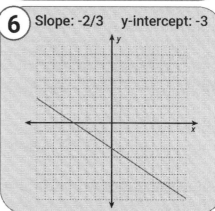

7 Slope: -5/6 y-intercept: -2

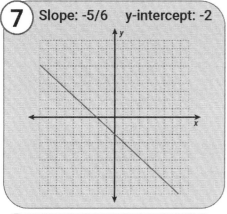

8 Slope: 1/2   y-intercept: 3

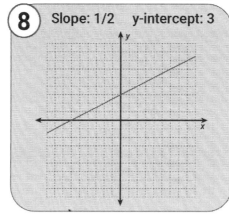

9 Slope: -1   y-intercept: 3

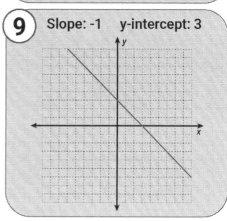

10 Slope: 1/2   y-intercept: -4

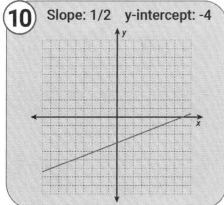

ANSWER EXPLANATIONS

Solving Linear Inequalities

1
-26 > -3x - 6 + 2x
-20 > -x
x > 20

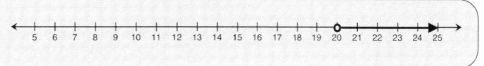

2
48 > 5x - 8 + 2x
56 > 7x
x < 8

3
3(6 - 2x) - 4x > 4x - 52
18 - 6x - 4x > 4x - 52
70 > 14x   x<5

4
5x - 146 < 2(3 - 5x) - 4x
5x - 146 < 6 - 10x - 4x
19x < 152   x < 8

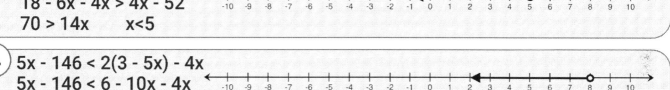

5
6x - 5 + 3x ≥ -77
9x ≥ -72
x ≥ -8

6
4(5 - 3x) < 9x - 64
20 - 12x < 9x - 64
84 < 21x   x > 4

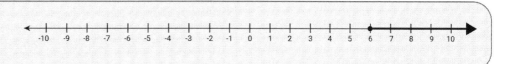

7
2(6 - 2x) ≤ 18 - 3(x + 4)
12 - 4x ≤ 18 - 3x - 12
x ≥ 6

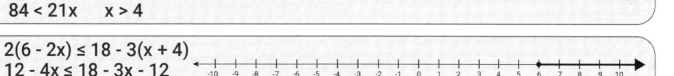

8
2(4 - 3x) ≥ 8x - 34
8 - 6x ≥ 8x - 34
14x ≤ 42   x ≤ 3

9
-5(1 - x) > 63 - 3(x + 4)
-5 + 5x > 63 - 3x - 12
8x > 56   x > 7

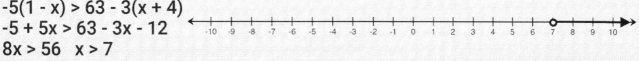

10
8(3 + 2x)- x > -3(x + 4)
24 + 16x - x > -3x - 12
x > -2

Simplifying Rational Expressions

(1) $\dfrac{(8a - 48)}{(a - 6)} = 8$

(2) $\dfrac{35}{5a - 45} = \dfrac{7}{a - 9}$

(3) $\dfrac{4a - 20}{24} = \dfrac{a - 5}{6}$

(4) $\dfrac{a - 2}{a^2 - 11a + 18} = \dfrac{1}{a - 9}$

(5) $\dfrac{15a^2}{5a^2} = 3$

(6) $\dfrac{a - 7}{a^2 + a - 56} = \dfrac{1}{a + 8}$

(7) $\dfrac{18a^3}{15a^3} = \dfrac{6}{5}$

(8) $\dfrac{5a + 40}{a + 8} = 5$

(9) $\dfrac{40a^4}{16a^4} = \dfrac{5}{2}$

(10) $\dfrac{10a^5}{25a^3} = \dfrac{2a^2}{5}$

(11) $\dfrac{15a^4}{20a^3} = \dfrac{3a}{4}$

(12) $\dfrac{a^2 + a - 2}{a - 1} = a + 2$

(13) $\dfrac{a^2 - 11a + 30}{a^2 - 2a - 35} = \dfrac{(a - 5)(a - 6)}{(a - 7)(a + 5)}$

(14) $\dfrac{a + 7}{a^2 + 13a + 42} = \dfrac{1}{a + 6}$

(15) $\dfrac{28a^2 + 42a + 14}{20a^2 - 22a - 16} = \dfrac{7(a + 1)}{5a - 8}$

(16) To simplify the given equation, the first step is to make all exponents positive by moving them to the opposite place in the fraction. This expression becomes:

$$\dfrac{4b^3b^2}{a^1a^4} \times \dfrac{3a}{b}$$

Then the rules for exponents can be used to simplify. Multiplying the same bases means the exponents can be added. Dividing the same bases means the exponents are subtracted.

(17) Simplify this to $(4a^2b^4)^{\frac{3}{2}} = 4^{\frac{3}{2}}(x^2)^{\frac{3}{2}}(y^2)^{\frac{3}{2}}$. Now $4^{\frac{3}{2}} = (\sqrt{4})^3 = 2^3 = 8$. For the other, recall that the exponents must be multiplied, so this yields
$$8a^{2\frac{3}{2}}b^{4\frac{3}{2}} = 8a^3b^6.$$

(18)

$$\dfrac{8a - 48}{a - 6} = \dfrac{8(a - 6)}{a - 6} = 8$$

ANSWER EXPLANATIONS

Adding and Subtracting Rational Expressions

(1) $\dfrac{4a^3 - 5b^2}{2a^4} + \dfrac{3a^3 + 3b^2}{2a^4} = \dfrac{7a^3 - 2b^2}{2a^4}$

(2) $\dfrac{3a^4 - 2b^5}{5a^5b^6} - \dfrac{3a^4 + 7b^5}{5a^5b^6} = \dfrac{-9}{5a^5b}$

(3) $\dfrac{7a^4}{4a^5 - 6} + \dfrac{3a^4 - 8}{4a^5 - 6} = \dfrac{5a^4 - 4}{2a^5 - 3}$

(4) $\dfrac{3a - 7}{5a^4 - 11a} + \dfrac{7a - 5}{5a^4 - 11a} = \dfrac{2(5a - 6)}{a(5a^2 - 11)}$

(5) $\dfrac{5a - 9}{2a^5 + 13a} - \dfrac{3a + 5}{2a^5 + 13a} = \dfrac{2(a - 7)}{g(2a^4 + 13)}$

(6) $\dfrac{4a^2 + 5b^2}{8a^3} + \dfrac{5a^2 - 6b^2}{8a^3} = \dfrac{9a^2 - b^2}{8a^3}$

(7) $\dfrac{8a - 9b}{6a^3b^2} - \dfrac{8a + 5b}{6a^3b^2} = \dfrac{-7}{3a^3b}$

(8) $\dfrac{a}{7} - \dfrac{4a + 1}{a + 3} = \dfrac{a^2 + 3a}{7a + 21} + \dfrac{28a + 7}{7a + 21} = \dfrac{a^2 - 25a - 7}{7a + 21} = \dfrac{a^2 - 25a - 7}{7(a + 3)}$

(9) $\dfrac{a}{3} + \dfrac{4a + 5}{a + 4} = \dfrac{a^2 + 4a}{3a + 12} + \dfrac{12a + 15}{3a + 12} = \dfrac{a^2 + 16a + 15}{3a + 12} = \dfrac{a^2 + 16a + 15}{3(a + 4)}$

(10) $\dfrac{4a}{6} + \dfrac{5a + 8}{3a + 9} = \dfrac{12a^2 + 36a}{18a + 54} + \dfrac{30a + 48}{18a + 54} = \dfrac{12a^2 + 66a + 48}{18a + 54} = \dfrac{2a^2 + 11a + 8}{3(a + 3)}$

Solving Rational Equations

(1) $x = 2$:

To solve for x the steps are as follows:

$4x - 12$

$-2x$, $6x - 12 = 0$

$6x = 12$

$x = 2$

(2) $x = \dfrac{1}{8}$

(3) $x = 39$

(4) $x = \dfrac{-1}{15}$

(5) $x = \dfrac{5}{77}$

ANSWER EXPLANATIONS

Factoring Quadratic Equations

1
$$x^2 - 9x = -20$$
Rewrite to add the c factor to the left side:
$$x^2 - 9x + 20 = 0$$
Factor by determining two numbers that have a sum equal to the coefficient of the b term and have a product equal to the c term:
$$(x - 4)(x - 5) = 0$$
Solve for x by setting each factor equal to zero:
$$x = 4, \text{ or } x = 5$$

2
$$x^2 + 2x = 35$$
Rewrite to add the c factor to the left side:
$$x^2 + 2x - 3520 = 0$$
Factor by determining two numbers that have a sum equal to the coefficient of the b term and have a product equal to the c term:
$$(x - 5)(x + 7) = 0$$
Solve for x by setting each factor equal to zero:
$$x = 5, \text{ or } x = -7$$

3
$$x^2 - 7x - 18 = 0$$
Factor by determining two numbers that have a sum equal to the coefficient of the b term and have a product equal to the c term:
$$(x - 9)(x + 2) = 0$$
Solve for x by setting each factor equal to zero:
$$x = 9, \text{ or } x = -2$$

4
$$x^2 + 8x = 20$$
Rewrite to add the c factor to the left side:
$$x^2 + 8x - 20 = 0$$
Factor by determining two numbers that have a sum equal to the coefficient of the b term and have a product equal to the c term:
$$(x + 10)(x - 2) = 0$$
Solve for x by setting each factor equal to zero:
$$x = -10, \text{ or } x = 2$$

ANSWER EXPLANATIONS

Factoring Quadratic Equations

5

$x^2 + 18x + 77 = 0$

Factor by determining two numbers that have a sum equal to the coefficient of the b term and have a product equal to the c term:

$(x + 7)(x + 11) = 0$

Solve for x by setting each factor equal to zero:

$x = -7$, or $x = -11$

6

$x^2 - 4x - 43 = 2$

Rewrite to add the c factor to the left side:

$x^2 - 4x - 45 = 0$

Factor by determining two numbers that have a sum equal to the coefficient of the b term and have a product equal to the c term:

$(x - 9)(x + 5) = 0$

Solve for x by setting each factor equal to zero:

$x = 9$, or $x = -5$

7

$x^2 + 5x - 24 = 0$

Factor by determining two numbers that have a sum equal to the coefficient of the b term and have a product equal to the c term:

$(x - 3)(x + 8) = 0$

Solve for x by setting each factor equal to zero:

$x = 3$, or $x = -8$

8

$x^2 + 17x = -72$

Rewrite to add the c factor to the left side:

$x^2 + 17x + 72 = 0$

Factor by determining two numbers that have a sum equal to the coefficient of the b term and have a product equal to the c term:

$(x + 9)(x + 8) = 0$

Solve for x by setting each factor equal to zero:

$x = -9$, or $x = -8$

ANSWER EXPLANATIONS

Factoring Quadratic Equations

9
$$6x^2 - 70x - 24 = 0$$
Factor by determining two numbers that have a sum equal to the coefficient of b term and have a product equal to the c term:
$$(6x + 2)(x - 12) = 0$$
Solve for x by setting each factor equal to zero:
$$x = -\frac{1}{3}, \text{ or } x = 12$$

10
$$x^2 + 22x + 120 = 0$$
Factor by determining two numbers that have a sum equal to the coefficient of b term and have a product equal to the c term:
$$(x + 10)(x + 12) = 0$$
Solve for x by setting each factor equal to zero:
$$x = -10, \text{ or } x = -12$$

11
$$x^2 - 3x = 88$$
Rewrite to add the c factor to the left side:
$$x^2 - 3x - 88 = 0$$
Factor by determining two numbers that have a sum equal to the coefficient of b term and have a product equal to the c term:
$$(x - 11)(x + 8) = 0$$
Solve for x by setting each factor equal to zero:
$$x = 11, \text{ or } x = -8$$

12
$$x^2 + 11x + 10 = 0$$
Factor by determining two numbers that have a sum equal to the coefficient of b term and have a product equal to the c term:
$$(x + 1)(x + 10) = 0$$
Solve for x by setting each factor equal to zero:
$$x = -1, \text{ or } x = -10$$

ANSWER EXPLANATIONS

Factoring Quadratic Equations

13

$6x^2 + 8x = 30$

Rewrite to add the c factor to the left side:

$6x^2 + 8x - 30 = 0$

Factor by determining two numbers that have a sum equal to the coefficient of the b term and have a product equal to the c term:

$(6x - 10)(x + 3) = 0$

Solve for x by setting each factor equal to zero:

$x = \dfrac{5}{3}$, or $x = -3$

14

$2x^2 - 13x = -15$

Rewrite to add the c factor to the left side:

$2x^2 - 13x + 15 = 0$

Factor by determining two numbers that have a sum equal to the coefficient of the b term and have a product equal to the c term:

$(2x - 3)(x - 5) = 0$

Solve for x by setting each factor equal to zero:

$x = \dfrac{3}{2}$, or $x = 5$

15

$4x^2 - 41x = 88$

Rewrite to add the c factor to the left side:

$4x^2 - 41x - 88 = 0$

Factor using the quadratic formula:

$$x = \frac{-b \pm \sqrt{b^2 - 4ac}}{2a} = \frac{41 \pm \sqrt{(-41)^2 - 4(4)(-88)}}{2(4)} = \frac{41 \pm \sqrt{3089}}{8}$$

Solving Quadratic Equations with the Quadratic Formula

1

$$x^2 + 2x - 35 = 0$$

For this quadratic equation, a = 1, b = 2, and c = -35.

Then, we simply plug these values into the quadratic formula: $x = \dfrac{-b \pm \sqrt{b^2 - 4ac}}{2a}$

$$x = \frac{-2 \pm \sqrt{2^2 - 4(1)(-35)}}{2(1)}$$

$$x = \frac{-2 \pm \sqrt{144}}{2}$$

$$x = \frac{-2 \pm 12}{2}$$

$$x = 5, \text{ or } x = -7$$

2

$$x^2 - 5x - 24 = 0$$

For this quadratic equation, a = 1, b = -5, and c = -24.

Then, we simply plug these values into the quadratic formula: $x = \dfrac{-b \pm \sqrt{b^2 - 4ac}}{2a}$

$$x = \frac{-(5) \pm \sqrt{(-5)^2 - 4(1)(-24)}}{2(1)}$$

$$x = \frac{5 \pm \sqrt{144}}{2}$$

$$x = \frac{5 \pm 11}{2}$$

$$x = 8, \text{ or } x = -3$$

3

$$x^2 + 3x - 54 = 0$$

For this quadratic equation, a = 1, b = 3, and c = -54.

Then, we simply plug these values into the quadratic formula: $x = \dfrac{-b \pm \sqrt{b^2 - 4ac}}{2a}$

$$x = \frac{-3 \pm \sqrt{3^2 - 4(1)(-54)}}{2(1)}$$

$$x = \frac{-2 \pm \sqrt{225}}{2}$$

$$x = \frac{-2 \pm 15}{2}$$

$$x = 6, \text{ or } x = -9$$

ANSWER EXPLANATIONS

Solving Quadratic Equations with the Quadratic Formula

④

$$x^2 - 16x + 63 = 0$$

For this quadratic equation, a = 1, b = -16, and c = 63.

Then, we simply plug these values into the quadratic formula: $x = \frac{-b \pm \sqrt{b^2 - 4ac}}{2a}$

$$x = \frac{-(-16) \pm \sqrt{(-16)^2 - 4(1)(63)}}{2(1)}$$

$$x = \frac{16 \pm \sqrt{256 - 252}}{2}$$

$$x = \frac{16 \pm 2}{2}$$

$$x = 9, \text{ or } x = 7$$

⑤

$$x^2 + 3x - 40 = 0$$

For this quadratic equation, a = 1, b = 3, and c = -40.

Then, we simply plug these values into the quadratic formula: $x = \frac{-b \pm \sqrt{b^2 - 4ac}}{2a}$

$$x = \frac{-3 \pm \sqrt{3^2 - 4(1)(-40)}}{2(1)}$$

$$x = \frac{-2 \pm \sqrt{169}}{2}$$

$$x = \frac{-2 \pm 13}{2}$$

$$x = 5, \text{ or } x = -8$$

⑥

$$x^2 - 2x - 120 = 0$$

For this quadratic equation, a = 1, b = -2, and c = -120.

Then, we simply plug these values into the quadratic formula: $x = \frac{-b \pm \sqrt{b^2 - 4ac}}{2a}$

$$x = \frac{-(-2) \pm \sqrt{(-2)^2 - 4(1)(-120)}}{2(1)}$$

$$x = \frac{2 \pm \sqrt{4 - (-480)}}{2}$$

$$x = \frac{2 \pm \sqrt{484}}{2}$$

$$x = \frac{2 \pm 22}{2}$$

$$x = 12, \text{ or } x = -10$$

ANSWER EXPLANATIONS

Solving Quadratic Equations with the Quadratic Formula

7)

$$x^2 - 20x - 96 = 0$$

For this quadratic equation, $a = 1$, $b = -20$, and $c = -96$.

Then, we simply plug these values into the quadratic formula: $x = \dfrac{-b \pm \sqrt{b^2 - 4ac}}{2a}$

$$x = \frac{-20 \pm \sqrt{(-20)^2 - 4(1)(-96)}}{2(1)}$$

$$x = \frac{-20 \pm \sqrt{784}}{2}$$

$$x = \frac{-20 \pm 28}{2}$$

$$x = 8, \text{ or } x = -24$$

8)

$$x^2 - 9x + 18 = 0$$

For this quadratic equation, $a = 1$, $b = -9$, and $c = 18$.

Then, we simply plug these values into the quadratic formula: $x = \dfrac{-b \pm \sqrt{b^2 - 4ac}}{2a}$

$$x = \frac{-(-9) \pm \sqrt{(-9)^2 - 4(1)(18)}}{2(1)}$$

$$x = \frac{9 \pm \sqrt{81 - 72}}{2}$$

$$x = \frac{9 \pm \sqrt{9}}{2}$$

$$x = \frac{9 \pm 3}{2}$$

$$x = 6, \text{ or } x = 3$$

9)

$$x^2 - 2x - 24 = 0$$

For this quadratic equation, $a = 1$, $b = -2$, and $c = -24$.

Then, we simply plug these values into the quadratic formula: $x = \dfrac{-b \pm \sqrt{b^2 - 4ac}}{2a}$

$$x = \frac{-(-2) \pm \sqrt{(-2)^2 - 4(1)(-24)}}{2(1)}$$

$$x = \frac{2 \pm \sqrt{4 - (-96)}}{2}$$

$$x = \frac{2 \pm \sqrt{100}}{2}$$

$$x = \frac{2 \pm 10}{2}$$

$$x = 6, \text{ or } x = -4$$

Solving Quadratic Equations with the Quadratic Formula

10

$$x^2 + 8x + 12 = 0$$

For this quadratic equation, a = 1, b = 8, and c = 12 .

Then, we simply plug these values into the quadratic formula: $x = \frac{-b \pm \sqrt{b^2 - 4ac}}{2a}$

$$x = \frac{-8 \pm \sqrt{8^2 - 4(1)(12)}}{2(1)}$$

$$x = \frac{-8 \pm \sqrt{16}}{2}$$

$$x = \frac{-8 \pm 4}{2}$$

x = -6, or x = -2

11

$$x^2 - 13x + 42 = 0$$

For this quadratic equation, a = 1, b = -13, and c = 42.

Then, we simply plug these values into the quadratic formula: $x = \frac{-b \pm \sqrt{b^2 - 4ac}}{2a}$

$$x = \frac{-(-13) \pm \sqrt{(-13)^2 - 4(1)(42)}}{2(1)}$$

$$x = \frac{13 \pm \sqrt{169 - 168}}{2}$$

$$x = \frac{13 \pm \sqrt{1}}{2}$$

$$x = \frac{13 \pm 1}{2}$$

x = 7, or x = 6

12

$$x^2 - 7x - 60 = 0$$

For this quadratic equation, a = 1, b = -7, and c = -60.

Then, we simply plug these values into the quadratic formula: $x = \frac{-b \pm \sqrt{b^2 - 4ac}}{2a}$

$$x = \frac{-(-7) \pm \sqrt{(-7)^2 - 4(1)(-60)}}{2(1)}$$

$$x = \frac{7 \pm \sqrt{49 - (-240)}}{2}$$

$$x = \frac{7 \pm \sqrt{289}}{2}$$

$$x = \frac{7 \pm 17}{2}$$

x = -5, or x = 12

ANSWER EXPLANATIONS

Solving Quadratic Equations with the Quadratic Formula

(13)
$$8x^2 - 32x - 40 = 0$$
For this quadratic equation, a = 8, b = -32, and c = -40.
Then, we simply plug these values into the quadratic formula: $x = \frac{-b \pm \sqrt{b^2 - 4ac}}{2a}$

$$x = \frac{-(-32) \pm \sqrt{(-32)^2 - 4(8)(40)}}{2(8)}$$

$$x = \frac{32 \pm \sqrt{1024 - (-1280)}}{16}$$

$$x = \frac{32 \pm \sqrt{2304}}{16}$$

$$x = \frac{32 \pm 48}{16}$$

$$x = -1, \text{ or } x = 5$$

(14)
$$18x^2 + 72x + 72 = 0$$
For this quadratic equation, a = 18, b = 72, and c = 72.
Then, we simply plug these values into the quadratic formula: $x = \frac{-b \pm \sqrt{b^2 - 4ac}}{2a}$

$$x = \frac{-72 \pm \sqrt{72^2 - 4(18)(72)}}{2(18)}$$

$$x = \frac{-72 \pm \sqrt{5184 - (5184)}}{36}$$

$$x = \frac{-72 \pm \sqrt{0}}{36}$$

$$x = \frac{-72 \pm 0}{36}$$

$$x = -2$$

(15)
$$12x^2 - 12x - 72 = 0$$
For this quadratic equation, a = 1, b = -12, and c = -72.
Then, we simply plug these values into the quadratic formula: $x = \frac{-b \pm \sqrt{b^2 - 4ac}}{2a}$

$$x = \frac{-(-12) \pm \sqrt{(-12)^2 - 4(12)(-72)}}{2(12)}$$

$$x = \frac{12 \pm \sqrt{144 - (-3456)}}{24}$$

$$x = \frac{12 \pm \sqrt{3600}}{24}$$

$$x = \frac{12 \pm 60}{24}$$

$$x = -2, \text{ or } x = 3$$

ANSWER EXPLANATIONS

Completing the Square

1
$$x^2 - 2x - 15 = 0$$
Add the c term to the other side of the equation: $x^2 - 2x = 15$
Divide the coefficient of b by 2, square the result, and add this quantity to both sides of the equation $(\frac{b}{2})^2$,
$$x^2 - 2x + 1 = 15 + 1$$
Factor the trinomial on the left side:
$$(x - 1)^2 = 16$$
Take the square root of both sides:
$$x - 1 = \pm\sqrt{16}$$
$x = 1 + 4 = 5$, and $x = 1 - 4 = -3$

2
$$x^2 + 2x = 35$$
Divide the coefficient of b by 2, square the result, and add this quantity to both sides of the equation $(\frac{b}{2})^2$,
$$x^2 + 2x + 1 = 35 + 1$$
Factor the trinomial on the left side:
$$(x + 1)^2 = 36$$
Take the square root of both sides:
$$x + 1 = \pm\sqrt{36}$$
$x = -1 + 6 = 5$, and $x = -1 - 6 = -7$

3
$$x^2 + 2x - 8 = 0$$
Add the c term to the other side of the equation: $x^2 + 2x = 8$
Divide the coefficient of b by 2, square the result, and add this quantity to both sides of the equation $(\frac{b}{2})^2$,
$$x^2 - 2x + 1 = 9$$
Factor the trinomial on the left side:
$$(x + 1)^2 = 9$$
Take the square root of both sides:
$$x + 1 = \pm\sqrt{9}$$
$x = -1 + 3 = 2$, and $x = -1 - 3 = -4$

4
$$x^2 + 10x + 7 = -2$$
Add the c term to the other side of the equation: $x^2 + 10x = -9$
Divide the coefficient of b by 2, square the result, and add this quantity to both sides of the equation $(\frac{b}{2})^2$,
$$x^2 + 10x + 25 = -9 + 25$$
Factor the trinomial on the left side:
$$(x + 5)^2 = 16$$
Take the square root of both sides:
$$x + 5 = \pm\sqrt{16}$$
$x = -5 + 4 = -1$, and $x = -5 - 4 = -9$

ANSWER EXPLANATIONS

Completing the Square

5 $x^2 - 8x - 20 = 0$. Add the c term to the other side of the equation: $x^2 - 8x = 20$
Divide the coefficient of b by 2, square the result, and add this quantity to both sides of the equation $(\frac{b}{2})^2$,
$x^2 - 8x + 16 = 20 + 16$
Factor the trinomial on the left side:
$(x - 41)^2 = 36$
Take the square root of both sides:
$x - 4 = \pm\sqrt{36}$
$x = 4 + 6 = 10$, and $x = 4 - 6 = -2$

6 $x^2 + 18x + 56 = 0$. Add the c term to the other side of the equation: $x^2 + 18x = -56$
Divide the coefficient of b by 2, square the result, and add this quantity to both sides of the equation $(\frac{b}{2})^2$,
$x^2 + 18x + 81 = -56 + 81$
Factor the trinomial on the left side:
$(x + 9)^2 = 25$
Take the square root of both sides:
$x + 9 = \pm\sqrt{25}$
$x = -9 + 5 = -4$, and $x = -9 - 5 = -14$

7 $x^2 - 6x - 55 = 0$. Add the c term to the other side of the equation: $x^2 - 6x = 55$
Divide the coefficient of b by 2, square the result, and add this quantity to both sides of the equation $(\frac{b}{2})^2$,
$x^2 - 6x + 9 = 55 + 9$
Factor the trinomial on the left side:
$(x + 3)^2 = 64$
Take the square root of both sides:
$x + 3 = \pm\sqrt{64}$
$x = -3 + 8 = 5$, and $x = -3 - 8 = -11$

8 $x^2 + 12x - 64 = 0$. Add the c term to the other side of the equation: $x^2 + 12x = 64$
Divide the coefficient of b by 2, square the result, and add this quantity to both sides of the equation $(\frac{b}{2})^2$,
$x^2 + 12x + 36 = 64 + 36$
Factor the trinomial on the left side:
$(x + 6)^2 = 100$
Take the square root of both sides:
$x + 6 = \pm\sqrt{100}$
$x = -6 + 10 = 4$, and $x = -6 - 10 = -16$

ANSWER EXPLANATIONS

Completing the Square

9 $x^2 + 8x + 7 = 0$. Add the c term to the other side of the equation: $x^2 + 8x = -7$

Divide the coefficient of b by 2, square the result, and add this quantity to both sides of the equation $(\frac{b}{2})^2$,

$$x^2 + 8x + 16 = -7 + 16$$

Factor the trinomial on the left side:

$$(x + 4)^2 = 9$$

Take the square root of both sides:

$$x + 4 = \pm\sqrt{9}$$

$$x = -4 + 3 = -1, \text{ and } x = -4 - 3 = -7$$

10 $x^2 - 19x + 90 = 0$. Add the c term to the other side of the equation: $x^2 - 19x = -90$

Divide the coefficient of b by 2, square the result, and add this quantity to both sides of the equation $(\frac{b}{2})^2$,

$$x^2 - 19x + \frac{361}{4} = -90 + \frac{361}{4}$$

Find a common denominator on the right side so that addition can be completed:

$$x^2 - 19x + \frac{361}{4} = -\frac{360}{4} + \frac{361}{4}$$

Add:

$$x^2 - 19x + \frac{361}{4} = \frac{1}{4}$$

Factor the trinomial on the left side:

$$(x - \frac{19}{2})^2 = \frac{1}{4}$$

Take the square root of both sides:

$$(x - \frac{19}{2})^2 = \pm\frac{1}{2}$$

$$x - \frac{19}{2} + \frac{1}{2} = \frac{20}{2} = 10 \text{ and } x = \frac{19}{2} - \frac{1}{2} = \frac{18}{2} = 9$$

11 $4x^2 - 12x - 4 = 12$. Divide the equation by the coefficient of a, which is 4, to get the leading

coefficient to be 1: $\frac{4x^2 - 12x - 4}{4} = \frac{12}{4} = x^2 - 3x - 1 = 3$

Add the c term to the other side of the equation: $x^2 - 3x = 4$

Divide the coefficient of b by 2, square the result, and add this quantity to both sides of the equation $(\frac{b}{2})^2$,

$$x^2 - 3x + \frac{9}{4} = 4 + \frac{9}{4}$$

Find a common denominator on the right side so that addition can be completed:

$$x^2 - 3x + \frac{9}{4} = \frac{16}{4} + \frac{9}{4}$$

Add:

$$x^2 - 3x + \frac{9}{4} = \frac{25}{4}$$

Factor the trinomial on the left side:

$$(x - \frac{3}{2})^2 = \frac{25}{4}$$

Take the square root of both sides:

$$x - \frac{3}{2} = \pm\frac{5}{2} \qquad x = \frac{3}{2} + \frac{5}{2} = \frac{8}{2} = 4 \text{ and } x = \frac{3}{2} - \frac{5}{2} = -\frac{2}{2} = -1$$

ANSWER EXPLANATIONS

Completing the Square

(12) $2x^2 - 22x + 60 = 0$. Divide the equation by the coefficient of a, which is 2, to get the leading coefficient to be 1: $\dfrac{2x^2 - 22x - 60}{2} = \dfrac{0}{2} = x^2 - 11x + 30 = 0$

Add the c term to the other side of the equation: $x^2 - 11x = -30$

Divide the coefficient of b by 2, square the result, and add this quantity to both sides of the equation $(\frac{b}{2})^2$

$$x^2 - 11x + \frac{121}{4} = -30 + \frac{121}{4}$$

Find a common denominator on the right side so that addition can be completed:

$$x^2 - 11x + \frac{121}{4} = -\frac{120}{4} + \frac{121}{4}$$

Add:

$$x^2 - 3x + \frac{121}{4} = \frac{1}{4}$$

Factor the trinomial on the left side:

$$(x - \frac{11}{2})^2 = \frac{1}{4}$$

Take the square root of both sides:

$$x - \frac{11}{2} = \pm\frac{1}{2} \qquad x = \frac{11}{2} + \frac{1}{2} = \frac{12}{2} = 6 \text{ and } x = \frac{11}{2} - \frac{1}{2} = \frac{10}{2} = 5$$

(13) $4x^2 + 8x + 22 = 0$. Divide the equation by the coefficient of a, which is 4, to get the leading coefficient to be 1: $\dfrac{4x^2 + 8x + 22}{4} = \dfrac{0}{4} = x^2 + 2x + \frac{11}{2} = 0$

Add the c term to the other side of the equation: $x^2 + 2x = -\dfrac{11}{2}$

Divide the coefficient of b by 2, square the result, and add this quantity to both sides of the equation $(\frac{b}{2})^2$

$$x^2 + 2x = -\frac{11}{2}$$

Find a common denominator on the right side so that addition can be completed:

$$x^2 + 2x + 1 = -\frac{4}{2} + 1$$

Add:

$$x^2 + 2x + 1 = -\frac{11}{2} + \frac{2}{2}$$

$$x^2 + 2x + 1 = -\frac{9}{2}$$

Factor the trinomial on the left side:

$$(x + 1)^2 = -\frac{9}{2}$$

Take the square root of both sides:

$$x + 1 = \pm\sqrt{\frac{9}{2}} \qquad x = 1 + \sqrt{\frac{9}{2}} \qquad x = 1 - \sqrt{\frac{9}{2}}$$

ANSWER EXPLANATIONS

Completing the Square

(14) $100x^2 - 100x - 9 = 0$. Divide the equation by the coefficient of a, which is 100, to get the leading coefficient to be 1: $\dfrac{100x^2 - 100x - 9}{100} = \dfrac{0}{100} = x^2 - x + \dfrac{9}{100} = 0$

Add the c term to the other side of the equation: $x^2 + x = \dfrac{9}{100}$

Divide the coefficient of b by 2, square the result, and add this quantity to both sides of the equation $\left(\dfrac{b}{2}\right)^2$

$$x^2 - x + \dfrac{1}{4} = \dfrac{9}{100} + \dfrac{1}{4}$$

Find a common denominator on the right side so that addition can be completed:

$$x^2 - x + \dfrac{1}{4} = \dfrac{9}{100} + \dfrac{25}{100}$$

Add:

$$x^2 - x + \dfrac{1}{4} = \dfrac{36}{100}$$

Factor the trinomial on the left side:

$$\left(x - \dfrac{1}{2}\right)^2 = \dfrac{36}{100}$$

Take the square root of both sides:

$x - \dfrac{1}{2} = \pm\dfrac{3}{5}$ $x = \dfrac{1}{2} + \dfrac{3}{5} = \dfrac{5}{10} + \dfrac{6}{10} = \dfrac{11}{10} = 1.1$ and $x = \dfrac{1}{2} - \dfrac{3}{5} = \dfrac{5}{10} - \dfrac{6}{10} = -\dfrac{1}{10} = -0.1$

(15) $12x^2 - 24x + 6 = -4$. Divide the equation by the coefficient of a, which is 12, to get the leading coefficient to be 1: $\dfrac{12x^2 - 24x + 6}{12} = -\dfrac{4}{12} = x^2 - 2x + \dfrac{6}{12} = -\dfrac{4}{12}$

Add the c term to the other side of the equation: $x^2 - 2x = -\dfrac{4}{12} - \dfrac{6}{12}$

Simplify:

$$x^2 - 2x = -\dfrac{5}{6}$$

Divide the coefficient of b by 2, square the result, and add this quantity to both sides of the equation $\left(\dfrac{b}{2}\right)^2$

$$x^2 - 2x + 1 = -\dfrac{5}{6} + 1$$

Simplify:

$$x^2 - 2x + 1 = \dfrac{1}{6}$$

Factor the trinomial on the left side:

$$(x - 1)^2 = \dfrac{1}{6}$$

Take the square root of both sides:

$x - 1 = \pm\, 0.408$ $x = 1 + 0.408 = 1.408$, and $x = 1 - 0.408 = 0.592$

ANSWER EXPLANATIONS

Solving Systems of Equations with Elimination

1

$3x + y = -21; x + y = -5$

Recall that solving systems of linear equations via the elimination method relies on the addition property of equality, which states that states that the same value can be added or subtracted to both sides of an equation and equality is maintained. Therefore, since x + y= -5, what's on the left (x+y) equals what is on the right (-5), so we can subtract the x + y to one side of our other equation and the -5 to the other, and we haven't changed the truth of the equality statement of our other equation.

$$3x + y = -21$$
$$-(x + y = -5)$$

$$2x + 0 = -16$$

Now, we can easily solve for x by dividing both sides by 2:

$$2x + 0 = -16$$
$$x = -8$$

Once we have our value for x, we can plug it in to either of the initial equations to solve for y:

$$x + y = -5$$
$$-8 + y = -5; y = 3$$

Therefore, the solution to the system is (-8, 3).

2

$-5x - 7y = 24; 10x + 7y = 1$

We can add these two equations to cancel out the y term:

$$-5x - 7y = 24$$
$$+ \quad 10x + 7y = 1$$

$$5x = 25$$

Solving for x yields x = 5

Next, we can plug in our calculated value for x into either equation to find y:

$$10x + 7y = 1$$
$$10(5) + 7y = 1$$
$$50 + 7y = 1$$
$$7y = -49$$
$$y = -7$$

Therefore, the solution to the system is (5, -7).

ANSWER EXPLANATIONS

Solving Systems of Equations with Elimination

3

$5x - 2y = 18$; $-2x - y = -9$

At first glance, it can be determined that these equations can't be simply added or subtracted to eliminate a variable. However, just as the addition property of equality can be used with the elimination method, so too can the multiplication property of equality, which states that the same non-zero real number can be multiplied by both sides of an equation without altering the truth of the equality statement of the original equation. Because division is the same as multiplying times a reciprocal, an equation can be divided by the same number on both sides as well. Therefore, we can multiply the second equation by -2 and then add the result to the first equation to cancel the y term:

$$-2(-2x - y = -9)$$
$$= 4x + 2y = 18$$

Now, we will add this result to the first equation, as doing so will cancel out the y term:

$$4x + 2y = 18$$
$$+ \quad 5x - 2y = 18$$
$$\text{-------------------------------}$$
$$9x = 36$$
$$x = 4$$

Next, we can plug in our calculated value for x into either equation to find y:

$$5x - 2y = 18$$
$$5(4) - 2y = 18$$
$$20 - 2y = 18$$
$$2y = 2$$
$$y = 1$$

Therefore, the solution to the system is (4, 1).

4

$x + 3y = 18$; $-x - 4y = -25$

We can add these two equations to cancel the x term:

$$x + 3y = 18$$
$$+ \quad -x - 4y = -25$$
$$\text{-------------------------------}$$
$$-y = -7$$
$$y = 7$$

Next, we can plug in our calculated value for y into either equation to find x:

$$x + 3y = 18$$
$$x + 3(7) = 18$$
$$x = -3$$

Therefore, the solution to the system is (-3, 7).

ANSWER EXPLANATIONS

Solving Systems of Equations with Elimination

⑤

$$y = -\frac{3}{2}x - 7; \quad y = \frac{1}{2}x + 5$$

Because both of these equations are equal to y, we can subtract one from the other to eliminate y:

$$y = \frac{1}{2}x + 5$$
$$- \quad y = -\frac{1}{2}x - 7$$
$$\text{------------------------------}$$
$$0 = \frac{4}{2}x + 12$$

Simplify:

$$-12 = 2x$$
$$x = -6$$

Next, we can plug in our calculated value for x into either equation to find y:

$$y = x + 5$$
$$y = \frac{1}{2}(-6) + 5$$
$$y = -3 + 5$$
$$y = 2$$

Therefore, the solution to the system is (-6, 2).

⑥

$$y = \frac{1}{4}x - 2; \quad y = -3x - 15$$

In this system, it is easiest to start by multiplying the first equation by 4 to get rid of the fraction:

$$4(y = \frac{1}{4}x - 2)$$
$$4y = x - 8$$

Now, we can multiply our result by 3 so that when we add the two equations, the x terms will cancel out:

$$3(4y = x - 8)$$
$$12y = 3x - 24$$

Add the two equations:

$$12y = 3x - 24$$
$$+ \quad y = -3x - 15$$
$$\text{------------------------------}$$
$$13y = -39$$
$$y = -3$$

Next, we can plug in our calculated value for y into either equation to find x:

$$y = -3x - 15$$
$$-3 = -3x - 15$$
$$3x = -12$$
$$x = -4$$

Therefore, the solution to the system is (-4, -3).

ANSWER EXPLANATIONS

Solving Systems of Equations with Elimination

7
$$y = -\frac{2}{7}x - 2; \; y = -\frac{1}{7}x - 4$$

Here, we can multiply both equations by 7 to get rid of the fractions:

$$7(y = -\frac{2}{7}x - 2) = 7y = -2x - 14$$
$$7(y = -\frac{1}{7}x - 4) = 7y = -x - 28$$

Next, we can subtract the second from the first:

$$7y = -2x - 14$$
$$- \quad 7y = -x - 28$$

$$0 = -x + 14$$
$$x = 14$$

Next, we can plug in our calculated value for x into either equation to find y:

$$y = -\frac{1}{7}x - 4$$
$$y = -\frac{1}{7}(14) - 4$$
$$y = -2 - 4$$
$$y = -6$$

Therefore, the solution to the system is (14, -6).

8
$$3x + 3y = -3; \; -3x - 4y = 2$$

These equations can be added to cancel the x term:

$$3x + 3y = -3$$
$$+ \; -3x - 4y = 2$$

$$-y = -1$$
$$y = 1$$

Next, we can plug in our calculated value for y into either equation to find x:

$$3x + 3y = -3$$
$$3x + 3(1) = -3$$
$$3x = -6$$
$$x = -2$$

Therefore, the solution to the system is (-2, 1).

ANSWER EXPLANATIONS

Solving Systems of Equations with Elimination

(9)

$-x + 2 = y$; $-6x - 3 = y$

Because both of these equations are equal to y, we can subtract one from the other to eliminate y:

$-x + 2 = y$

$- \quad -6x - 3 = y$

$5x + 5 = 0$

$x = -1$

Next, we can plug in our calculated value for y into either equation to find x:

$-x + 2 = y$

$-(-1) + 2 = y$

$y = 3$

Therefore, the solution to the system is (-1, 3).

(10)

$4x - y = -1$; $-3x + 2y = -3$

For this system, multiplying the first equation by 2 and then adding it to the second equation will cancel out the y term:

$2(4x - y = -1)$

$8x - 2y = -2$

Now, we add the two equations:

$8x - 2y = -2$

$+ \quad -3x + 2y = -3$

$5x = -5$

$x = -1$

Next, we can plug in our calculated value for x into either equation to find y:

$4x - y = -1$

$4(-1) - y = -1$

$y = -3$

Therefore, the solution to the system is (-1, -3).

ANSWER EXPLANATIONS

Solving Systems of Equations with Substitution

1

$$y = 4x - 10; \quad y = \frac{1}{3}x + 1$$

Because both of the given equations are equal to y, we can set them equal to one another to solve for x. Therefore, $4x - 10 = \frac{1}{3}x + 1$. To solve for x, we need to isolate the variable by moving all instances of x to one side of the equation. However, in this case, since we have a fraction of x on one side, it makes sense to remove the fraction by multiplying all terms by the reciprocal:

$$3(4x - 10) = 3(\frac{1}{3}x + 1)$$

$$12x - 30 = x + 3$$

Then, we can simplify:

$$11x = 33$$

Solving for x yields:

$$x = 3$$

Next, we substitute the calculated value of x into either of the initial equations to solve for y:

$$y = 4(3) - 10$$

$$y = 12 - 10 = 2$$

For completeness, it can be seen that the other equation would yield the same value for y:

$$y = \frac{1}{3}(3) + 1$$

$$y = 1 + 1 = 2$$

Therefore, the solution is (3, 2).

2

$$y = 4x + 5; \quad y = -\frac{1}{3}x - 8$$

Because both of the given equations are equal to y, we can set them equal to one another to solve for x. Therefore, $4x + 5 = -\frac{1}{3}x - 8$. To solve for x, we need to isolate the variable by moving all instances of x to one side of the equation. However, in this case, since we have a fraction of x on one side, it makes sense to remove the fraction by multiplying all terms by the reciprocal:

$$3(4x + 5) = 3(-\frac{1}{3}x - 8)$$

$$12x + 15 = -x - 24$$

Then, we can simplify:

$$13x = -39$$

Solving for x yields:

$$x = -3$$

Next, we substitute the calculated value of x into either of the initial equations to solve for y:

$$y = 4(-3) + 5$$

$$y = -12 + 5 = -7$$

Therefore, the solution is (-3, -7).

ANSWER EXPLANATIONS

Solving Systems of Equations with Substitution

3

$$y = -4x + 15; \quad y = -\frac{7}{2}x + 12$$

Because both of the given equations are equal to y, we can set them equal to one another to solve for x. Therefore, $-4x + 15 = -\frac{7}{2}x + 12$. To solve for x, we need to isolate the variable by moving all instances of x to one side of the equation. However, in this case, since we have a fraction of x on one side, it makes sense to remove the fraction by multiplying all terms by the reciprocal:

$$2(-4x + 15) = 2(-\frac{7}{2}x + 12)$$

$$-8x + 30 = -7x + 24$$

Then, we can simplify:

$$6 = x$$

Next, we substitute the calculated value of x into either of the initial equations to solve for y:

$$y = -4(6) + 15$$

$$y = -24 + 15 = -9$$

Therefore, the solution is (6, -9).

4

$$2x - 3y = -1; \quad -x + y = -1$$

First, we need to solve one of the equations in terms of the other. That seems easier with the second equation:

$$-x + y = -1$$

$$y = x - 1$$

Now, we can substitute this equation in for y in our other equation, because it will enable us to have only one variable— x—in that equation.

$$2x - 3y = -1$$

$$2x - 3(x - 1) = -1$$

Distribute:

$$2x - 3x + 3 = -1$$

Next, we simplify by isolating the variable on one side of the equation and the constants on the other:

$$-x = -4$$

Therefore, x = 4.

Next, we substitute the calculated value of x into the equation we manipulated to be in terms of y:

$$y = x - 1$$

$$y = 4 - 1 = 3$$

Therefore, the solution is (4, 3).

ANSWER EXPLANATIONS

Solving Systems of Equations with Substitution

5

$$y = \frac{1}{2}x + 4; \quad y = -\frac{5}{2}x + 10$$

Because both of the given equations are equal to y, we can set them equal to one another to solve for x. Therefore, $\frac{1}{2}x + 4 = -\frac{5}{2}x + 10$. To solve for x, we need to isolate the variable by moving all instances of x to one side of the equation. However, in this case, since we have a fraction of x on one side, it makes sense to remove the fraction by multiplying all terms by the reciprocal:

$$2(\frac{1}{2}x + 4) = 2(-\frac{5}{2}x + 10)$$

$$x + 8 = -5x + 20$$

Then, we can simplify:

$$6x = 12$$

Solving for x yields:

$$x = 2$$

Next, we substitute the calculated value of x into either of the initial equations to solve for y:

$$y = \frac{1}{2}(2) + 4$$

$$y = 1 + 4 = 5$$

Therefore, the solution is (2, 5).

6

$$-16 = 8x + y; \quad -3x + y = -5$$

First, we need to solve one of the equations in terms of the other. We will use the first equation:

$$-16 = 8x + y$$

$$y = -8x - 16$$

Now, we can substitute this equation in for y in our other equation, because it will enable us to have only one variable—x—in that equation.

$$-3x + y = -5$$

$$-3x + (-8x - 16) = -5$$

Next, we simplify by isolating the variable on one side of the equation and the constants on the other:

$$11x = -11$$

Therefore, x = -1.

Next, we substitute the calculated value of x into the equation we manipulated to be in terms of y:

$$y = -8x - 16$$

$$y = -8(-1) - 16$$

$$y = 8 - 16, \quad y = -8$$

Therefore, the solution is (-1, -8).

ANSWER EXPLANATIONS

Solving Systems of Equations with Substitution

(7)

$5x + 2y = 21; -x - y = -9$

First, we need to solve one of the equations in terms of the other. We will use the second equation:

$-x - y = -9$

$y = 9 - x$

Now, we can substitute this equation in for y in our other equation, because it will enable us to have only one variable —x— in that equation.

$5x + 2y = 21$

$5x + 2(9 - x) = 21$

Distribute:

$5x + 18 - 2x = 21$

Next, we simplify by isolating the variable on one side of the equation and the constants on the other:

$3x = 3$

Therefore, $x = 1$.

Next, we substitute the calculated value of x into the equation we manipulated to be in terms of y:

$y = 9 - x$

$y = 9 - 1; y = 8$

Therefore, the solution is (1, 8).

(8)

$6x - 5y = 12; 2x + y = 20$

First, we need to solve one of the equations in terms of the other. We will use the second equation to solve for y:

$2x + y = 20$

$y = 20 - 2x$

Now, we can substitute this equation in for y in our other equation, because it will enable us to have only one variable—x—in that equation:

$6x - 5y = 12$

$6x - 5(20 - 2x) = 12$

Distribute:

$6x - 100 + 10x = 12$

Next, we simplify by isolating the variable on one side of the equation and the constants on the other:

$112 = 16x$

Therefore, $x = 7$.

Next, we substitute the calculated value of x into the equation we manipulated to be in terms of y:

$y = 20 - 2x$

$y = 20 - 2(7)$

$y = 20 - 14 = 6$

Therefore, the solution is (7, 6).

ANSWER EXPLANATIONS

Solving Systems of Equations with Substitution

(9)

$$5 = 4x - 7y; 9x - 7y = -15$$

Because both of the given equations have a -7y term, we can rearrange them and set them equal to one another:

$$5 = 4x - 7y$$

$$5 - 4x = -7y$$

And:

$$9x - 7y = -15$$

$$-7y = -15 - 9x$$

Therefore:

$$5 - 4x = -15 - 9x$$

Now, we can simplify:

$$5x = -20, x = -4$$

Now, we can substitute this equation in for x in either equation to find the value of y:

$$5 = 4(-4) - 7y$$

$$5 = -16 - 7y$$

$$21 = -7y; y = -3$$

Therefore, the solution is (-4, -3).

(10)

$$y = -\frac{7}{5}x - 3; y = -\frac{4}{9}x - 3$$

Because both of the given equations are equal to y, we can set them equal to one another to solve for x. Therefore, $-\frac{7}{5}x - 3 = -\frac{4}{9}x - 3$. To solve for x, we need to isolate the variable by moving all instances of x to one side of the equation. However, in this case, since we have a fraction of x on both sides, we need to find a common denominator:

$$-\frac{7}{5}x - 3 = -\frac{4}{9}x - 3$$

$$-\frac{63}{45}x - 3 = -\frac{20}{45}x - 3$$

Then, we can simplify by moving the x terms to one side of the equation and the constants to the other:

$$\frac{43}{45}x = 0$$

Then, we can simplify by solving for x:

$$x = 0$$

Next, we substitute the calculated value of x into either of the initial equations to solve for y, which is -3.

Therefore, the solution is (0, -3).

ANSWER EXPLANATIONS

Using Formulas

1 **210 miles**: All we need to do to find the distance is to plug the provided values for the rate and time into the formula:

$d = r \times t$

$d = 35 \text{ mph} \times 6 \text{ hours}$

$d = 210 \text{ miles}$

2 **26.7 degrees C**:
See the calculation below:

$C = \frac{5}{9}(F - 32)$

$C = \frac{5}{9}(80 - 32)$

$C = \frac{5}{9}(48)$

$C = 26.7 \text{ degrees}$

3 **6 cm**: The formula for the perimeter of a rectangle is P=2L+2W, where P is the perimeter, L is the length, and W is the width.

The first step is to substitute all of the data into the formula:

$36 = 2(12) + 2W$

Simplify by multiplying 2 × 12:

$36 = 24 + 2W$

Simplifying this further by subtracting 24 on each side, which gives:

$36 - 24 = 24 - 24 + 2W$

$12 = 2W$

Divide by 2:

$6 = W$

The width is 6 cm. Remember to test this answer by substituting this value into the original formula:

$36 = 2(12) + 2(6)$

4 **36 sq. mm**: All we need to do for this problem is plug the provided values into our formula: $\frac{1}{2}bh$

$\frac{1}{2}(6)(12) = 36 \text{ square mm}$

5 **12 inches**: See the calculations below:

$13^2 = 5^2 + b^2$

$13^2 - 5^2 = b^2$

$169 - 25 = b^2$

$144 = b^2$

$b = 12 \text{ inches}$

6 **1080 degrees**: An octagon has 8 sides. Therefore, the sum of the internal angles is:

$= 180(n-2)$

$= 180(8-2)$

$= 180(6)$

$= 1080 \text{ degrees}$

ANSWER EXPLANATIONS

Using Formulas

(7) **5 inches and 7 inches**: This problem involves a manipulating the formula a little. We know the area of a trapezoid can be calculated using the formula: $A = \frac{1}{2} \times h(b_1 + b_2)$, where h is the height and b_1 and b_2 are the parallel bases of the trapezoid. We also know that in our trapezoid, one base is 2 inches longer than the other. Therefore, we can rewrite $b_1 + b_2$ to be expressed in relation to one another: $b_1 + (b_1 + 2)$, which can be simplified to $2b_1 + 2$.

Then, we can substitute this into our original formula:

$$A = \frac{1}{2} \times h(b_1 + b_2)$$
$$A = \frac{1}{2} \times h(2b_1 + 2)$$

Next, we can plug in the values we know:

$$A = \frac{1}{2} \times h(2b_1 + 2)$$
$$24 = \frac{1}{2} \times 4(2b_1 + 2)$$

Now we can simplify and rearrange the formula to isolate our missing variable.

We can start by multiplying the ½ and 4:

$$24 = 2(2b_1 + 2)$$

Next, divide both sides by 2:

$$12 = (2b_1 + 2)$$

Subtract 2 from both sides:

$$10 = 2b_1$$

Divide both sides by 2:

$$b_1 = 5$$

Now, we know that the shorter of the two bases is 5 inches, so the longer base is 5 + 2 = 7 inches. We can check our answer by plugging these lengths into the area formula:

$$A = \frac{1}{2} \times h(b_1 + b_2)$$
$$A = \frac{1}{2} \times 4(5 + 7)$$
$$A = \frac{1}{2} \times 4(12)$$
$$A = 24 \text{ square inches}$$

(8) **5 inches**: Here is another example where we need to manipulate the formula to isolate our variable of interest. We know that the formula for the surface area of a rectangular prism is:

$$SA = 2xy + 2yz + 2xz$$

Plugging in the values we know yields:

$$SA = 2xy + 2yz + 2xz$$
$$184 = 2(8)(4) + 2(4)(z) + 2(8)(z)$$

Simplifying like terms:

$$184 = 64 + 8z + 16z$$
$$120 = 24z$$
$$z = 5 \text{ inches}$$

Again, we can check this by substituting it into our formula:

$$SA = 2xy + 2yz + 2xz$$
$$SA = 2(8)(4) + 2(4)(5) + 2(8)(5)$$
$$SA = 184 \text{ square inches}$$

ANSWER EXPLANATIONS

Using Formulas

9 **54 square cm:** This problem requires two main steps. First, we have to solve for the side length of the cube using the volume formula:

$$V = s \times s \times s = s^3$$
$$27 = s^3$$

Taking the cube root of both sides yields s = 3 cm.
Next, we need to plug this value into the surface area formula:

$$SA = 6s^2$$
$$SA = 6(3)^2$$
$$SA = 6 \times 9$$
$$SA = 54 \text{ square cm.}$$

10 **Pentagon with 8 cm sides:** To solve this problem, we should start by using the internal angle formula to find the number of sides, and thus the identity:

$$540 = 180(n - 2)$$
$$3 = n - 2$$
$$n = 5$$

Therefore, we are working with a pentagon. Next, we can use the formula and the values provided to solve for the perimeter. From there, we can determine the side length:

$$A = \frac{1}{2} \times a \times P$$
$$120 = \frac{1}{2} \times 6 \times P$$

Simplify:

$$120 = 3p$$

Divide both sides by 3:

$$40 = P$$

Next, we know that the formula for the perimeter of a pentagon is:

$$P = 5s$$

We can plug in our value of P to solve for s:

$$40 = P = 5s$$
$$s = 8cm$$

ANSWER EXPLANATIONS

Writing Equations to Model Situations

1 $y = 40x + 50,000$: For manufacturing costs, there is a linear relationship between the cost to the company and the number produced, with a y-intercept given by the base cost of acquiring the means of production, and a slope given by the cost to produce one unit. In this case, that base cost is $50,000, while the cost per unit is $40.
So, $y = 40x + 50,000$.

2 $2l + 2(l - 2) = 44$: The first step is to determine the unknown, which is in terms of the length, l.
The second step is to translate the problem into the equation using the perimeter of a rectangle, $P = 2l + 2w$. The width is the length minus 2 centimeters. The resulting equation is $2l + 2(l - 2) = 44$. The equation can be solved as follows:

$2l + 2l - 4 = 44$	Apply the distributive property on the left side of the equation
$4l - 4 = 44$	Combine like terms on the left side of the equation
$4l = 48$	Add 4 to both sides of the equation
$l = 12$	Divide both sides of the equation by 4

The length of the rectangle is 12 centimeters. The width is the length minus 2 centimeters, which is 10 centimeters. Checking the answers for length and width forms the following equation:
$$44 = 2(12) + 2(10)$$
The equation can be solved using the order of operations to form a true statement:
$$44 = 44.$$

3 $c = 15g + 20p + 10$. In this equation, the cost of the phone bill per month is represented by c, and g represents the gigabytes of data used that month, while p represents the number of active phone lines.

ANSWER EXPLANATIONS

Algebraic Word Problems

(1) **6:** This problem involved setting up an algebraic equation to solve for x, or the number of flower trays Carly purchased. The equation is as follows:

$$6x + 8x = 84$$
So,
$$14x = 84$$
Then divide each side by 14 to solve for x:
$$x = \frac{84}{14} = 6 \text{ trays}$$

(2) **8:** Let a be the number of apples and b the number of bananas. Then, the total cost is $2a + 3b = 22$, while it also known that $a + b = 10$. Using the knowledge of systems of equations, cancel the b variables by multiplying the second equation by -3. This makes the equation $-3a - 3b = -30$. Adding this to the first equation, the b values cancel to get $-a = -8$, which simplifies to $a = 8$.

(3) **4:** Let r be the number of red cans and b be the number of blue cans. One equation is $r + b = 10$. The total price is $16, and the prices for each can means $1r + 2b = 16$. Multiplying the first equation on both sides by -1 results in $-r - b = -10$. Add this equation to the second equation, leaving $b = 6$. So, she bought 6 blue cans. From the first equation, this means $r = 4$; thus, she bought 4 red cans.

(4) **20 yo-yos:** Let y be the number of initial yo-yos in his collection. We can write the following equation from the given information:

$$16 = 6 + \frac{1}{2}y$$
Then we solve for y:
$$10 = \frac{1}{2}y$$
$$y = 20 \text{ yo-yos}$$

(5) **47:** We can represent the pages in the book relative to one another. The lowest page number can be p. Then, the next consecutive page is $p + 1$, and the third page is $p + 2$. Therefore, we can write the following equation using only one letter variable:

$$144 = p + (p + 1) + (p + 2)$$
Simplifying and solving yields:
$$144 = 3p + 3$$
$$141 = 3p$$
$$p = 47$$
Thus, the lowest page is 47, then the other two are 48 and 49.

ANSWER EXPLANATIONS

Algebraic Word Problems

6   **43 tickets**: Let t be the number of tickets she had before buying the football. Then, we can write the following equation from the given information:

$$26 = \frac{t + 9}{2}$$

Simplifying and solving yields:

$$26 = \frac{t + 9}{2}$$
$$52 = t + 9$$
$$t = 43 \text{ tickets}$$

7   **$17**: Let c be the cost of each poster. First, we can figure out how much he spent on the posters:

$$\$165 - \$29 = \$136$$

Then, we can write the following equation from the given information:

$$\$136 = 8c$$
$$c = \$17$$

8   **46 students**: Let s be the number of students per bus. First, we can figure out the number of students who rode a bus:

$$331 - 9 = 322 \text{ students}$$

Then, we can write the following equation from the given information:

$$322 = 7s$$
$$s = 46 \text{ students}$$

9   **$9**: Let t be the cost of each ticket. Thus, we can write the following equation:

$$13 = \frac{12 + 3t}{3}$$

Simplifying and solving yields:

$$39 = 12 + 3t$$
$$27 = 3t$$
$$t = \$9$$

10   **33 cups**: First, we have to determine the profit on each cup of lemonade sold. To do this, we start by determining the cost of ingredients per cup. Because each pitcher makes 8 cups, we divide the cost per pitcher by 8: $1.12 / 8 = $.14 per cup. Then we can determine the profit per cup: $0.75 - $0.14 = $0.61 per cup profit. Then, to determine the number of cups she needs to sell: $20.00 / $0.61 = 32.8. This needs to be rounded up to 33 cups because she can only sell whole cups.

ANSWER EXPLANATIONS

Algebraic Word Problems

(11) **174 bottles:** This problem requires two equations and two variables. Let's let c be the number of aluminum cans and b be the number of glass bottles. Then we can write the following:

$$29.00 = .05c + .10b$$

And:

$$b = \frac{3}{4}c$$

Therefore, we can substitute this value of b into our first equation to eliminate one of the variables:

$$29.00 = .05c + .10\left(\frac{3}{4}c\right)$$
$$29.00 = .125c$$
$$c = 232$$

Therefore, they had 232 cans. To find the number of bottles, we can then use our second equation:

$$b = \frac{3}{4}c$$
$$b = \frac{3}{4}(232)$$
$$b = 174$$

(12) **5 batches:** Again, we need two variables and two equations here. Let b be the number of brownie batches and c be the number of cookie batches. Therefore, we can write the following equations from the provided information:

$$184 = 16b + 24c$$
$$c = b + 1$$

Then, we can substitute this value of c relative to b into our first equation to eliminate one variable:

$$184 = 16b + 24c$$
$$184 = 16b + 24(b + 1)$$

Simplifying and solving yields:

$$184 = 16b + 24(b + 1)$$
$$184 = 16b + 24b + 24$$
$$160 = 40b$$
$$b = 4$$

This means that she baked 4 batches of brownies. Since she baked one more batch of cookies than brownies, she baked 5 batches of cookies.

ANSWER EXPLANATIONS

Algebraic Word Problems

(13) **33 games:** This problem can be solved easily by dividing 44 by 4 (which is 11). This means ¼ of the games, 11 games, are home games. Therefore, the remainder (44 − 11 = 33 games) are away games.

(14) **9 ladybugs:** This is another instance where we can write two equations and use two variables, and then rewrite one variable in terms of the other so that we can solve for one of the variables. We will define l as the number of lady bugs and s as the number of spiders. Because ladybugs are insects, they have six legs, and spiders have eight legs. Therefore, we know the total number of legs (198) is equal to six legs per ladybug times the number of ladybugs plus eight legs per spider times the number of spiders. We also know there are twice as many spiders as ladybugs. Thus, the following equations can be written in this problem:

$$198 = 6l + 8s$$
$$s = 2l$$

Then, we can substitute this value of s relative to l into our first equation to eliminate one variable:

$$198 = 6l + 8s$$
$$198 = 6l + 8(2l)$$

Simplifying and solving yields:

$$198 = 6l + 16l$$
$$198 = 22l$$
$$l = 9$$

Therefore, she counts 9 ladybugs. For completeness, since she counts twice as many spiders as ladybugs, she counts 9 x 2 = 18 spiders. This can be checked by plugging these values into the initial equation:

$$198 = 6(9) + 8(18)$$
$$198 = 54 + 144$$
$$198 = 198$$

(15) **28 students:** This is another relatively simple problem. If there are seven groups with four students each, there are 4 x 7 = 28 students in the class.

(16) **59.5 minutes:** To solve this rate problem, we first need to determine Shankar's pace per mile in his five-mile run. To do this, we divide the total time by 5 miles. 42:30 is equal to 42.5 minutes, since 30 seconds is equal to half of one minute. Thus:

$$\frac{42.5 \text{ min}}{5 \text{ miles}} = 8.5 \text{ min/mile}$$

Next, we multiply this pace by 7 to find the time it will take him to run 7 miles:

$$8.5 \frac{\text{min}}{\text{mile}} \times 7 \text{ miles} = 59.5 \text{ minutes} = 59 \text{ minutes and } 30 \text{ seconds}$$

ANSWER EXPLANATIONS

Algebraic Word Problems

(17) **5 days**: This is another instance where we can write two equations and use two variables, and then rewrite one variable in terms of the other so that we can solve for one of the variables. We will define l as the number of long days (50 minutes) and s as the number of short days of practice (30 minutes). Because long days are 50 minutes and short days are 30 minutes, we know that the total number of weekly minutes is equal to the number of long days (l) times 50 minutes per (l) day plus the number of short days (s) times 30 minutes per short day. We also know the sum of the number of l and s days is seven since there are seven days in a week. First, we need to convert the weekly time to minutes so that all times have the same units:

$$5 \text{ hours} \times 60 \frac{min}{hour} + 10 \text{ min} = 310 \text{ min}$$

Now we can write our two equations:

$$310 = 50l + 30s$$
$$7 = l + s$$

Next, we can write the second equation in terms of one variable relative to the other:

$$l = 7 - s$$

Now, we can substitute this value of l into our first equation so that we only have one variable to deal with:

$$310 = 50l + 30s$$
$$310 = 50(7 - s) + 30s$$

Simplifying and solving yields:

$$310 = 50(7 - s) + 30s$$
$$310 = 350 - 50s + 30s$$
$$40 = 20s$$
$$s = 2 \text{ days}$$

Therefore, 2 of the days are her shorter 30-minute sessions, which means that 5 days are spent playing 50 minutes since there are 7 days in a week.

(18) **33 hours**: Since we know that her total earnings ($396) is comprised of 1/3 tips and 2/3 of her wages, we can multiply $396 by 2/3 to find the earnings from her wages alone:

$$\$396 \times \frac{2}{3} = \$264$$

Therefore, Sam's mom earned $264 from her wages. Since she makes 8 dollars an hour, we can divide this amount by 8 to find the number of hours worked:

$$\frac{\$264}{\$8/hr} = 33 \text{ hours}$$

ANSWER EXPLANATIONS

Algebraic Word Problems

(19) **$324**: This problem may seem daunting at first, but we can write an equation with the information we know. She babysat 6 times. Five of those times were four hours and one was six hours. Of the five four-hour times, four were $12 per hour and one was $15 per hour because it had an extra child.
Therefore, we can write and solve the following equation:

$$\text{Total earnings} = 4(4 \times \$12) + (4 \times \$15) + (6 \times \$12)$$
$$= 4(\$48) + \$60 + \$72$$
$$= \$192 + \$60 + \$72$$
$$= \$324$$

(20) **6 boxes**: The team needs a total of $270, and each box earns them $3. Therefore, the total number of boxes needed to be sold is 270 ÷ 3, which is 90. With 15 people on the team, the total of 90 can be divided by 15, which equals 6. This means that each member of the team needs to sell 6 boxes for the team to raise enough money to buy new uniforms.

(21) **30 oranges**: One apple/orange pair costs $3 total. Therefore, Jan bought 90 ÷ 3 = 30 total pairs, and hence, she bought 30 oranges.

(22) **4**: Kristen bought four DVDs, which would cost a total of 4 × 15 = $60. She spent a total of $100, so she spent $100 - $60 = $40 on CDs. Since they cost $10 each, she must have purchased 40 ÷ 10 = 4 CDs.

(23) **390**: Three girls for every two boys can be expressed as a ratio: 3:2. This can be visualized as splitting the school into 5 groups: 3 girl groups and 2 boy groups. The number of students that are in each group can be found by dividing the total number of students by 5: 650 divided by 5 equals 1 part, or 130 students per group. To find the total number of girls, the number of students per group (130) is multiplied by how the number of girl groups in the school (3). This equals 390.

(24) **$62**: Kimberley worked 4.5 hours at the rate of $10/h and 1 hour at the rate of $12/h. The problem states that her pay is rounded to the nearest hour, so the 4.5 hours would round up to 5 hours at the rate of $10/h. 5 × $10 + 1 × $12 = $50 + $12 = $62.

ANSWER EXPLANATIONS

Algebraic Word Problems

25 **$0.45:** To solve this problem, list the givens:

Store coffee = $1.23/lbs

Local roaster coffee = $1.98/1.5 lbs

Calculate the cost for 5 lbs. of store brand.

$$\frac{\$1.23}{1 \text{ lbs}} \times 5 \text{ lbs} = \$6.15$$

Calculate the cost for 5 lbs. of the local roaster.

$$\frac{\$1.98}{1.5 \text{ lbs}} \times 5 \text{ lbs} = \$6.60$$

Subtract to find the difference in price for 5 lbs.

$$\begin{array}{r} \$6.60 \\ -\$6.15 \\ \hline \$0.45 \end{array}$$

26 **$3,325:** List the givens.

1,800 ft. = $2,000

Cost after 1,800 ft. = $1.00/ft.

Find how many feet left after the first 1,800 ft.

$$\begin{array}{r} 3,125 \text{ ft.} \\ -\ 1,800 \text{ ft.} \\ \hline 1,325 \text{ ft.} \end{array}$$

Calculate the cost for the feet over 1,800 ft.

$$1,325 \text{ ft.} \times \frac{\$1.00}{1 \text{ ft}} = \$1,325$$

Total for entire cost.

$2,000 + $1,325 = $3,325

27 **18:** If Ray will be 25 in three years, then he is currently 22. The problem states that Lisa is 13 years younger than Ray, so she must be 9. Sam's age is twice that, which means that the correct answer is 18.

28 **35 feet:** Denote the width as w and the length as l. Then, l = 3w + 5. The perimeter is 2w + 2l = 90. Substituting the first expression for l into the second equation yields 2(3w + 5) + 2w = 90, or 8w = 80, so w = 10. Putting this into the first equation, it yields l = 3(10) + 5 = 35 feet.

ANSWER EXPLANATIONS

Functions
Domain and Range

1
{(7,2), (6,6), (-2,4), (2,5), (-6,2)}
Function? Yes
Domain: {-6,-2,2,6,7}
Range: {2,4,5,6}

2
{(3,3), (1,9), (2,8), (-7,4), (6,7)}
Function? Yes
Domain: {-7,1,2,3,6}
Range: {3,4,7,8,9}

3
{(4,8), (5,1), (2,6), (-2,-8), (2,-6)}
Function? No
Domain: {-2,2,4,5}
Range: {-8,-6,1,6,8}

4
{(-9,- 8), (5,5), (7,7), (2,3), (1,-5)}
Function? Yes
Domain: {-9,1,2,5,7}
Range: {-8,-5,3,5,7}

5
{(-3,-5), (2,-8), (8,5), (-1,-7), (2,-8)}
Function? No
Domain: {-3,-1,2,8}
Range: {-8,-7,-5,5}

6
{(-1,-4), (-3,-6), (-6,-1), (-7,1), (-9,-3)}
Function? Yes
Domain: {-9,-7,-6,-3,-1}
Range: {-6,-4,-3,-1,1}

7
{(-2,7), (5,-1), (-4,-3), (-2,2), (3,6)}
Function? No
Domain: {-4,-2,3,5}
Range: {-3,-1,2,6,7}

8
{(-4,9), (5,8), (4,-5), (-3,-2), (8,-3)}
Function? Yes
Domain: {-4,-3,4,5,8}
Range: {-5,-3,-2,8,9}

9
{(-9,-2), (-2,-8), (-6,-3), (-2,0), (2,-3)}
Function? No
Domain: {-9,-6,-2,2}
Range: {-8,-5,-3,-2,0}

10
{(-9,-7), (6,-2), (-5,2), (-9,-8), (-7,-9)}
Function? No
Domain: {-9,-7,-5,6}
Range: {-9,-8,-2,2}

11
{(6,5), (-6,9), (4,3), (6,4), (-7,-8)}
Function? No
Domain: {-7,-6,4,6}
Range: {-8,3,4,5,9}

12
{(7,-1), (8,5), (1,5), (7,-1), (-9,4)}
Function? No
Domain: {-9,1,7,8}
Range: {-1,4,5}

13
{(-9,0), (0,1), (-8,-9), (-1,-2), (1,-8)}
Function? No
Domain:{-9,-8,-1,0,1}
Range: {-9,-8,-2,0,1}

14
{(4,2), (-9,1), (-3,0), (-1,5), (4,-7)}
Function? No
Domain: {-9,-3,-1,4}
Range: {-7,0,1,2,5}

15
(7,7), (2,-1), (-5,4), (-6,6), (-7,4)}
Function? Yes
Domain: {-7,-6,-5,2,7}
Range: {-1,4,6,7}

16
{(3,2), (2,2), (-5,2), (0,2), (-2,2)}
Function? Yes
Domain: {-5,-2,0,2,3}
Range: {2}

ANSWER EXPLANATIONS

Functions
Complete the Input/Output Table

(1) $f(x) = x^2 - 3$

x	f(x)
-2	1
-1	-2
0	-3
1	-2
2	1

(2) $f(x) = 2x + 4$

x	f(x)
-2	0
-1	2
1	6
2	8
5	14

(3) $f(x) = 5x^2 - 1$

x	f(x)
-3	44
-1	4
2	19
3	44
5	124

(4) $f(x) = 8 - 5x$

x	f(x)
-6	38
-3	23
0	8
3	-7
5	-17

(5) $f(x) = -3x + 6$

x	f(x)
-5	21
-1	9
0	6
5	-9
7	-15

(6) $f(x) = x^2 - 2$

x	f(x)
-4	14
-3	7
0	-2
1	-1
2	2

ANSWER EXPLANATIONS

Functions
Complete the Input/Output Table

7 $f(x) = 3 - 2x$

x	$f(x)$
-3	9
-1	5
0	3
2	-1
4	-5

8 $f(x) = 2x^3$

x	$f(x)$
-2	-16
-1	-2
1	2
2	16
3	54

9 $f(x) = \frac{x}{3}$

x	$f(x)$
-6	-2
-3	-1
3	1
6	2
9	3

10 $f(x) = \frac{x^3}{2}$

x	$f(x)$
-2	-4
1	0.5
2	4
3	13.5
4	32

Composite Functions

1 **-2**: As with all problems in this exercise, this problem involves a composition function, where one function is plugged into the other function. In this case, the $f(x)$ function is plugged into the $g(x)$ function for each x-value. The composition equation becomes $g(f(x)) = 2^3 - 3(2^2) - 2(2) + 6$. Simplifying the equation gives the answer $g(f(x)) = 8 - 3(4) - 2(2) + 6 = 8 - 12 - 4 + 6 = -2$.

2 x - 6

3 x -12

4 8 - 5x

5 x + 1

6 10x + 10

7 2(x - 1)

8 2x-19

9 9x - 23

10 -2x - 9

11 29 - 9x

12 x - 4

13 x - 18

14 5x-46

15 2x

16 -112 - 72x

17 9(4x - 5)

18 8x + 34

19 126x - 33

20 21x + 94

ANSWER EXPLANATIONS

Putting It All Together

1 **D:** The slope is given by the change in y divided by the change in x. Specifically, it's:

$$\text{slope} = \frac{y_2 - y_1}{x_2 - x_1}$$

The first point is (-5, -3) and the second point is (0, -1). Work from left to right when identifying coordinates. Thus, the point on the left is point 1 (-5, -3), and the point on the right is point 2 (0, -1).

Now we need to just plug those numbers into the equation:

$$\text{slope} = \frac{-1 - (-3)}{0 - (-5)}$$

It can be simplified to:

$$\text{slope} = \frac{-1 + 3}{0 + 5}$$

$$\text{slope} = \frac{2}{5}$$

2 **B:** To be directly proportional means that y = mx. If x is changed from 5 to 20, the value of x is multiplied by 4. Applying the same rule to the y-value, also multiplies the value of y by 4. Therefore, y = 12.

3 **B:** From the slope-intercept form, y = mx + b, it is known that b is the y-intercept, which is 1. Compute the slope as $\frac{2 - 1}{1 - 0}$ = 1, so the equation should be y = x + 1.

4 **A:** Each bag contributes 4x + 1 treats. The total treats will be in the form 4nx + n where n is the total number of bags. The total is in the form 60x + 15, from which it is known n = 15.

5 **D:** 34. When performing calculations consisting of more than one operation, the order of operations should be followed: Parenthesis, Exponents, Multiplication/Division, Addition/Subtraction.

Parenthesis:

$7^2 - 3 \times (4 + 2) + 15 \div 5$

$7^2 - 3 \times (6) + 15 \div 5$

Exponents:

$7^2 - 3 \times 6 + 15 \div 5$

$49 - 3 \times 6 + 15 \div 5$

Multiplication/Division (from left to right):

$49 - 3 \times 6 + 15 \div 5$

$49 - 18 + 3$

Addition/Subtraction (from left to right):

$49 - 18 + 3 = 34$

ANSWER EXPLANATIONS

Putting It All Together

6 **A:** Finding the roots means finding the values of x when y is zero. The quadratic formula could be used, but in this case, it is possible to factor by hand, since the numbers -1 and 2 add to 1 and multiply to -2. So, factor $x^2 + x - 2 = (x - 1)(x + 2) = 0$, then set each factor equal to zero. Solving for each value gives the values $x = 1$ and $x = -2$.

7 **C:** To find the y-intercept, substitute zero for x, which gives us:
$$y = 0^{\frac{5}{3}} + (0 - 3)(0 + 1)$$
$$0 + (-3)(1) = -3$$

8 **A:** This has the form $t^2 - y^2$, with $t = x^2$ and $y = 4$. It's also known that $t^2 - y^2 = (t + y)(t - y)$, and substituting the values for t and y into the right-hand side gives:
$$(x^2 - 4)(x^2 + 4)$$

9 **A:** First solve for x, y, and z.
So: $3x = 24$
$$x = 8$$
$$6y = 24$$
$$y = 4$$
$$-2z = 24$$
$$z = -12$$
This means the equation would be $4(8)(4) + (-12)$, which equals 116.

10 **B:** $\dfrac{5}{2} \div \dfrac{1}{3} = \dfrac{5}{2} \times \dfrac{3}{1} = \dfrac{15}{2} = 7.5$

11 **A:** The solid dot is located between -2 and -3, and the open dot is located between 1 and 2. Therefore, x is between -2.5 and 1.5, which can be converted to $-\dfrac{5}{2}$ and $\dfrac{3}{2}$. The solid dot indicates greater than or equal to, and the open dot indicates less than so the inequality is:
$$-\dfrac{5}{2} \le x < \dfrac{3}{2}$$

12 **B:** To simplify this inequality, subtract 3 from both sides to get $-\dfrac{1}{2}x \ge -1$. Then, multiply both sides by -2 (remembering this flips the direction of the inequality) to get $x \le 2$.

13 **A:** The slope is given by: $\text{slope} = \dfrac{y_2 - y_1}{x_2 - x_1} = \dfrac{0 - 4}{0 - (-3)} = -\dfrac{4}{3}$

ANSWER EXPLANATIONS

Putting It All Together

(14) **A:** The expression in the denominator can be factored into the two binomials $(x - 4)(x - 2)$. Once the expression is rewritten as $\frac{x-4}{(x-4)(x-2)}$, the values of $x = 4$ and $x = 2$ result in a denominator with a value of 0. Since 0 cannot be in the denominator of a fraction, the expression is undefined at the values of $x = 2, 4$.

(15) **A:** The first step is to find the equation of the line that is perpendicular to $y = 2x - 3$ and passes through the point $(0,5)$. The slope of a perpendicular line is found by the negative reciprocal of 2, which is $-\frac{1}{2}$. The y-intercept is the value of y when $x = 0$, so the y-intercept is 5. The new equation is:
$$y = -\frac{1}{2}x + 5$$
In order to find which points lie on the new line, the values of x and y can be substituted into the equation to determine if they form a true statement. For A, the equation $4 = -\frac{1}{2}(2) + 5$ makes a true statement, so the point $(2, 4)$ lies on the lines. For B, the equation $7 = -\frac{1}{2}(-2) + 5$ makes the statement $7 = 6$, which is not a true statement. Therefore, B is not a point that lies on the line. For C, the equation $-3 = -\frac{1}{2}(4) + 5$ becomes $-3 = 3$ which is not a true statement, so the point $(4, -3)$ is not on the line. For the last point in D, the equation $10 = -\frac{1}{2}(-6) + 5$ makes the statement $10 = 8$. This is not a true statement, so the point $(-6, 10)$ does not lie on the line.

(16) **B:** To factor $x^2 + 4x + 4$, the numbers needed are those that add to 4 and multiply to 4. Therefore, both numbers must be 2, and the expression factors to:
$$x^2 + 4x + 4 = (x + 2)^2$$
Similarly, the expression factors to $x^2 - x - 6 = (x - 3)(x + 2)$, so that they have $x + 2$ in common.

(17) **D:** This system of equations involves one quadratic function and one linear function, as seen from the degree of each equation. One way to solve this is through substitution. Solving for y in the second equation yields $y = x + 2$. Plugging this equation in for the y of the quadratic equation yields $x^2 - 2x + x + 2 = 8$. Simplifying the equation, it becomes $x^2 - x + 2 = 8$. Setting this equal to zero and factoring, it becomes:
$$x^2 - x - 6 = 0 = (x - 3)(x + 2)$$
Solving these two factors for x gives the zeros $x = 3, -2$. To find the y-value for the point, each number can be plugged in to either original equation. Solving each one for y yields the points $(3, 5)$ and $(-2, 0)$.

ANSWER EXPLANATIONS

Putting It All Together

18) **B:** The y-intercept of an equation is found where the x-value is zero. Plugging zero into the equation for x, the first two terms cancel out, leaving -4.

19) **D:** 3 times the sum of a number and 7 is greater than or equal to 32 can be translated into equation form utilizing mathematical operators and numbers.

20) **B:** The number line shows:
$$x > -\frac{3}{4}$$
Each inequality must be solved for x to determine if it matches the number line. Choice A of $4x + 5 < 8$ results in $x < -\frac{3}{4}$, which is incorrect. Choice C of $-4x + 5 > 8$ yields $x < -\frac{3}{4}$, which is also incorrect. Choice D of $4x - 5 > 8$ results in $x > \frac{13}{4}$, which is not correct. Choice B, $-4x + 5 < 8$ is the only choice that results in the correct answer of:
$$x > -\frac{3}{4}$$

21) **C:** The equation used to find the slope of a line when given two points is as follows:
$$slope = \frac{y_2 - y_1}{x_2 - x_1}$$
Substituting the points into the equation yields:
$$\frac{8 - (-4)}{-5 - 10}$$
$$\frac{12}{-15}$$
$$-\frac{4}{5}$$

22) **B:** The system can be solved using substitution. Solve the second equation for y, resulting in $y = 1 - 2x$. Plugging this into the first equation results in the quadratic equation $x^2 - 2x + 1 = 4$. In standard form, this equation is equivalent to $x^2 - 2x - 3 = 0$ and in factored form is $(x - 3)(x + 1) = 0$. Its solutions are $x = 3$ and $x = -1$. Plugging these values into the second equation results in $y = -5$ and $y = 3$, respectively. Therefore, the solutions are the ordered pairs (-1, 3) and (3, -5).

23) **B:** The function presented is being evaluated for $x + 1$; therefore, $x + 1$ must be substituted into the original function as follows:
$$f(x + 1) = (x + 1)^2 - 3(x + 1) + 17$$
The squared portion of the function becomes $x^2 + 2x + 1$, and distributing the -3 results in:
$$f(x + 1) = x^2 + 2x + 1 - 3x - 3 + 17$$
Combining like terms results in:
$$x^2 - x + 15$$

Made in the USA
Columbia, SC
27 March 2025

55753993R00067